Solo

Inspirational
cooking for one

Linda Tubby

Photography by Ali Allen

Kyle Books

This book of recipes is full of the food that I like to eat
and is dedicated to my lovely sons Dan and Ben, my mum Lou,
godmum Dodo and all my friends and family who enjoy eating.

First published in Great Britain in 2015 by
Kyle Books
an imprint of Kyle Cathie Limited
192–198 Vauxhall Bridge Road
London SW1V 1DX
general.enquiries@kylebooks.com
www.kylebooks.com

10 9 8 7 6 5 4 3 2 1

ISBN: 978 0 85783 278 8

A CIP catalogue record for this title is available from the British Library

Linda Tubby is hereby identified as the author of this work in accordance with Section 77 of the Copyright, Designs and Patents Act 1988.

Text © Linda Tubby 2015
Photographs © Ali Allen 2015
Design © Kyle Books 2015

Editor: Vicky Orchard
Photography and Styling: Ali Allen
Food Styling: Linda Tubby
Production: Gemma John and Nic Jones

Colour reproduction by ALTA London
Printed and bound in China by Toppan Leefung Printing Ltd

CONTENTS

INTRODUCTION

'People seldom do what they believe in.
They do what is convenient then repent.'

Bob Dylan

for ourselves what most of us have a deep desire to do for others. Cooking for yourself is a most satisfying part of self-nurture; when thought and care are given to the process, from shopping for ingredients to preparing a meal, you can take great pleasure in eating the results. In essence, feeding oneself can provide an experience that can bring a more confident solo existence along with happiness and contentment. The ethos and the recipes within this book are an attempt to inspire just that.

Most people I know eat a reasonable diet and love to make their food a considered part of a daily routine. But when stressed and very hungry, all of us have experienced panic eating, usually turning to unhealthy foods. We swoop on what will fill us up quickly with the least possible work. So it's time to transform cooking solo into an exciting creative experience so that meals aren't just viewed as quick fuel, grabbed to eat on the run, but a means to nurture yourself as many days of the week as you can manage.

Y ou may be one of the fast rising number of people living as one, renting in shared accommodation, a carnivore living with a vegan or maybe just occasionally catering solo. No matter what brings you here, this book no longer means you have to subsist on endless leftover dinners and cold takeaway food.

Being given the chance to prepare, cook and eat solo can bring life-affirming independence. It's all about how we take responsibility to do

Many of us love to entertain: the joy of seeing friends and family and cooking lovely things for everyone to enjoy. Yet I have to admit on such occasions a mildly selfish thought spins into my mind that a delicious treat or two will be had from the pickings of such efforts the next day. So I always overdo the cooking on these occasions to ensure I have at least one no-prep meal on hand sometime soon. I also use this thought as a motivational tool if I'm finding cooking solo a chore. I cook recipes for me to eat myself as practice ready for next time I cook for family or friends. Remember you have no obligations except to yourself, so experiment – you don't need to feel pressured into getting it right first time. Call it creative therapy, relaxation or just a bit of fun.

All the recipes are geared towards cooking the *Solo* way. Of course, the quantities for all of them can be doubled to serve two or three depending on how many dishes you decide to cook. Be mindful when seasoning and spicing the dishes, and don't increase these vital ingredients without tasting, tasting, tasting – let your instincts be your guide.

SET A MOOD OF TRANQUILLITY

'Always lay a table' was my Granny Tilly's mantra; she reigned over hers. It gives such a good feeling to sit down to dine solo at a beautifully laid table with a linen cloth and napkin. I hear screams of iron involvement but there's no need for that. If you can also manage a beautiful view as you eat then you will feel all the better for it: a balcony loaded with greenery to look out onto, a tiny garden with things you care for and love, all arranged how you like them and with colours that please you. Or simply a vase of flowers or a bowl of perfect eggs will add to the mood. As a solo diner it's up to you when, where and how, but mealtimes need to be as tranquil as possible in order to properly savour and digest. While this is not always easy to achieve on a daily basis, at least try it out sometimes during the course of your week.

How we choose to self-nurture through the food we eat is a conscious choice we all need to make to be healthy. We should all be having regular meals, when hungry it helps to make sure you feed yourself well. Without advocating gluttony, this is perhaps an obvious statement but segues neatly into pointing out this is not a diet book, simply a way of eating well.

I'm personally not always practising constant mindfulness in what I choose to turn into a meal. I am overly fond of sweet things, I sometimes indulge, pig out, feast extravagantly. Often I buy and eat frugally, buy rubbish, buy wisely, I eat healthily, I pick. In fact, I cover the range, but in general I seek balance; I pay attention to what my body doesn't like, and I think about food a lot. In general I cook and eat well but more fundamentally I enjoy the entire process. I hope you will too.

DON'T EVER FEEL BAD ABOUT LICKING YOUR PLATE

After some years working in India I got happily accustomed to eating with my fingers and I can recommend the technique for solo eating, not just to save on washing up but also to enjoy the tactile experience. You can even give yourself permission to lick your plate too, because no one will ever know! Imagine the most umami tastes still puddling on your plate, you have already gone in with the spoon but it's not yet clean ... how can you resist?

Solo isn't just about super-fast or shortcut meals to instantly sate the appetite (even though that aspect is covered), it's about being creative and getting great food on the table to give maximum satisfaction, not just in the eating but also in how you arrive there. I cross-reference ingredients to recipes so you can utilise any excess. And the exact same meal need not be repeated or anything go to waste.

Bringing joy into your life is important, so saying 'I can't be bothered' or 'I'll do that later' should no longer be an option. With the exception of course, if you find yourself truly, madly stretched. Try entering the mindset that if you do make that extra push and put a little more energy into getting that meal to your table it will make you feel better about everything. Your life will become less stressful and you will begin to feel relaxed knowing you have made the next meal a little easier and so enjoy it much more.

'Sow the seeds of something wonderful.'

ENJOY WELL-CHOSEN INGREDIENTS

I personally prefer to buy organic but if you have to manage on a small budget then do what you can. Growing organically provides essential habitat for important wildlife. Without the bees our own future could be affected. It's important we get a regular update on the ever-changing debate regarding GM products in animal feed and the use of antibiotics as growth promoters, as well as who is allowing GM crops to be grown and where. We need to be aware what is coming into our food chain without our knowledge. Be mindful this is not the natural way and we may regret such interference at some time in the future.

So long as you are happy with the provenance of the animal and the way it has been reared, then certainly use it. It's the same with vegetables and fish – it's best to focus on foods that are fresh and have not been hanging around for too long. Fresh, local foods are best. Be inspired by the changing seasons as delicious fresh produce comes to market.

It takes no time to sow some fennel seeds in your garden or in pots on the balcony. Growing things yourself will give so much inspiration and ultimate satisfaction. You can harvest their vivid green fronds, flowers, pollen and seeds and if lucky enough the roots. Try as well to plant lots of different herbs and salad leaves. Sow mizuna, two types of rocket, nasturtiums and borage. Micro leaves are wonderful too; the more you grow the better to add flourish to your dishes.

Plant some flowers to add colour to salads. Buy a tray of mixed coloured tiny viola plants in flower. Cut off all the flowering stems as you don't know if they've been sprayed or where they've been: water the plants well then transplant into a few pots. Within a week you will have re-grown pretty, fresh flowers.

'Put a handful of flowering fennel in a creamy stone pot to enjoy.'

THE BENEFITS: A FEW GUILTY PLEASURES

Foods to enjoy on your own can lift your spirits when food shopping, so be extravagant occasionally. A tiny jar of caviar with wafer-thin toasted sourdough if that takes your fancy or a whole lobster to serve with *Salmoriglio* (page 89). Some beautiful, fresh langoustine to steam and serve with a good mayonnaise or a few thin slices of calf's liver with sage from the garden, a tranche of turbot or half a dozen oysters. What nicer way to end a hard day? For me, the perfect finale would be a small sliver of flourless homemade cake with fruit, coconut yogurt and a dusting of fruit powder.

Don't feel guilty about making a sweet treat for a weekly indulgence, after all, you know the quality of your ingredients, and some crisp *Meringue shards* (page 219) or *Pecan and maple syrup spongy cake* (page 163) will finish off a simple supper very nicely.

I do buy excellent mayonnaise off the shelf, to save time, but having it in my fridge wouldn't stop me making my own if the mood takes me. Buy burrata, that naughty but nice mozzarella ball with a savoury, salty, double cream centre. But if it's tricky to get hold of, a good-quality buffalo mozzarella is good to use, bearing in mind next time you find yourself in that tempting Italian deli en route home, you will try burrata. Serve it broken into oozing chaos over fresh garden peas boiled for seconds, some bitter grilled radicchio or over the *Pea and lemon risotto with shimeji mushrooms* on page 170.

SETTING UP YOUR STORE CUPBOARD

Cooking the recipes in *Solo* you will gradually build up a supply of store cupboard ingredients from the essential to the quirky. I tend to use the same storable ingredients over and over, but now and again I see something in a specialist shop or online that makes me have to buy it to experiment with and add to my collection. Rather than having too much of one ingredient, sitting on my shelf unloved for years and turning stale, I share it with friends and do a swap for some home-grown produce or some hugs.

> If you have organised a few useful ingredients for your cupboards and shelves, fridge and freezer, you can rest assured that you don't always have to think what the next meal will be. You don't need much to make a comforting meal, maybe some good-quality canned tuna, black rice noodles and the addition of a homemade tomato sauce; it's ready in minutes so you can throw in a few handfuls of spinach and scatter over some toasted pine nuts to finish the dish.

I didn't set out to be over-prescriptive about what to buy for the store cupboard, but within the chapters you will find a number of my favourite ingredients that I use constantly and always have on my shelf. Useful things like pul biber pepper flakes (also known as Aleppo pepper), sumac, Espelette pepper, pistachio nibs, peppery extra virgin olive oil, Cornish sea salt crystals, saba and white balsamic vinegar. All the dry ingredients I use in the recipes such as black rice noodles, farro, freekeh and quinoa will store well in a mouse-proof cupboard or a drawer. Think Beatrix Potter – you don't want them dropping in to steal your stash!

'Let colour be your taste inspiration.'

GET CREATIVE WITH UNUSUAL SHELF INGREDIENTS

These are those nice bits and pieces that bring inspiration when looking to perk up to your dishes. Quirky ingredients can be the essential battery pack to boost your solo repertoire. A jar of rose petals, deep purple urfa pepper, black lava, pink Himalayan and Salish salts, barberries or even some home-pickled nasturtium seeds can be the start of your culinary box of tricks. The idea is to glam-up your food with visually creative and tasty additions, taking a meal that may be ordinary at first glance into a new dimension, making it not only taste good but look good too.

Use your local open-all-hours shops, ethnic grocers and specialist delis on the way home. On their shelves you might discover some intriguing ingredients that you're often unsure what to do with. Many tasty bits can be found for the jaded evening traveller perhaps intent on a big glass of vino on arriving home. Well, you can have one of those while the *Freekeh* (page 130) softens or the *Maftoul* (page 112) cooks and you can happily skin your tomatoes as you nibble on the best olives.

Make the most of free-foraged gems to pep up your recipes. Look to the seasons to inspire: when the elderflowers are blooming get out with friends to pick from trees that you sense will be as pollution free as possible and make batches of cordial to use in a variety of recipes, from sorbet to salad dressing. Wild garlic can be used for all sorts of dishes and is the best prize of all.

As our personal space becomes increasingly more important and how we look verging on the obsessive, we perhaps need to take a good look at how we eat. We cut corners to the detriment of taste and pleasure by continually shopping in the wrong places, buying too many 'convenient' non-essentials. I'm all for cheating a bit but not to the extent of involving anything other than simple pure ingredients.

When you love flavour and you have the best seasonal ingredients around you there's no need to do too much to them. A fillet of beautiful fish, small home-grown early potatoes with freshly podded peas and beans and some great salted Normandy butter, all that's required is that they're cooked to perfection. There is always the temptation to do more, but when your ingredients are all glowingly fresh and they taste great why gild the lily, and what could be quicker?

'You can't fake quality any more than you can fake a good meal.'

———

William S. Burroughs

GET PREPARED

You have a blank page when catering solo, with only yourself to satisfy. It can be daunting, but as Aristotle said: 'Happiness is a state of activity'. Keep this in mind and have some fun. Make patience part of your daily practice, especially as you come to the weekend, and enjoy the moments of cooking in preparation for the week ahead.

If you can't manage to do everything, then at least try to do something. I'm not advocating filling the freezer, just a little *mise en place* – chef's speak for preparing ahead. After your weekly shop, prepare as much as possible while you have the energy and creative buzz. Then value the calmness that organising your food needs for the week ahead will bring. The love a cook gives to food in its preparation is important as it can make it not only something that sustains and gives satisfaction but can be a little bit of creative therapy too.

Take 30 minutes or so to prepare a few useful bits to add to your basic meals for the coming week from the A Little Ahead and Those Little Extras chapters. For those who think life is too short to crush garlic then my task is to convert you. Don't waste money on jars of ready crushed stuff, to me the biggest heresy, taking all the pleasure away from the joy of cooking. I use a lot of garlic and it gives me a sense of satisfaction making a whole batch of crushed garlic paste in advance (see page 207). Make a pot of *Rich tomato sauce* to last up to four days (page 127), toast enough pine nuts for the week (page 200), prepare some *Crispy shallots* (page 202) and a few portions of farro and *Puy lentils* (pages 84 and 121). Then if time is really short all you need is some fresh fish or a steak and some lovely fresh seasonal vegetables and you have a meal that will bring a smile to your face.

I admit I love to cook and I'm an enthusiastic diner. I also love the organising so when it comes to the eating bit I feel relaxed having been sort of in control! Think about what your taste buds fancy before embarking on shopping for fresh produce and groceries. Although, you may change your mind in the course of a week it's a good idea to get a feeling of anticipation flowing. Try to work out how many evening meals you may need, barring surprise invites or friends dropping by.

The best piece of advice I was given that saves time when you get home tired and ready to cook, is to boil a kettle of water. Not just by way of a swift cuppa but to have the water ready to steam your vegetables or boil those potatoes.

STORING

It is important to take time with the immediate storage of your ingredients: give them the respect they deserve, bringing value to the precious food we can take for granted. This ultimately lightens the load when a meal is being prepared at a later date. Even though getting home on a Saturday lunchtime loaded with shopping bags of perishables can be daunting and enough to make anyone announce 'the weekend starts here' and reach for a large glass of something cold and interesting.

Having bought a few meats you might fancy for the days ahead you need to get them out of their packaging right away. Put each into non-corrosive dishes, grind over freshly ground black pepper, perhaps smear with crushed garlic, add a good slug of delicious oil, tuck in branches of thyme or rosemary. Cover the dishes and put in the fridge. Turn every day and they will keep and tenderise for up to three days or more, ready to turn into the recipe you choose. A piece of chunky fish sprinkled with sea salt as soon as it's home will help preserve it for a couple of days. Bear in mind you can eat half a portion of anything you have bought right away. Rinse watercress and salad leaves and layer between kitchen paper in a container and put in the fridge, this way they last for longer. If you grow your own, always put into water right after picking to keep them fresh then layer and store as above.

THE PRACTICAL BIT

The essential fridge...

This book sets out with as little complication as possible to address the issue solo diners hate the most – waste. From a financial and ethical point of view we all want to avoid it. If your fridge works well there will be no problem keeping food for three or more days whether fresh, marinated, lightly salted or cooked. Just be sure to keep raw meat and fish on the lowest shelf and always make sure cooked food is given enough time to cool completely before storing. The reverse applies if you're cooking something from the fridge: you will need to bring it to room temperature first, especially solid pieces of meat. Also any cooked food eaten straight from the fridge isn't as tasty – cold dulls flavour.

A really useful way to cool cooked food down quickly, ready for storing, is to put it in a container (without covering) and sit it in a basin of cold water that comes halfway up the sides. When cold, pop the lid on and store in the fridge, or freeze if you have to.

Storing food can be a challenge so don't overuse or crowd your fridge with things that are best cooked with, or consumed, at room temperature. For me it's pure sacrilege keeping every single fruit and vegetable in the fridge where flavour is compromised and nothing continues to ripen. Instead enjoy their beauty, make lovely displays of produce that will last out of the fridge, such as apples, pears and citrus fruits. Onions and garlic look great in containers that allow a little air to circulate. A cold larder or an airy under-the-stairs cupboard is ideal, even a box with a mesh front on a balcony is better for storing fruit and vegetables. Just keep foods away from radiators and out of constant sunlight of course. Soft fruits and fragile vegetables and salads are better off in the colder environment of your fridge alongside all the obvious things that need to be there in order not to go bad and toxic.

Fresh eggs don't need to be fridge cold, instead either leave in their boxes, with the top taken off, which looks great in the kitchen or pile them into your favourite bowl, which can be used as a table decoration instead of flowers.

Potatoes should never be kept in the fridge as being too cold converts the starch to sugar more quickly, affecting the flavour, texture and how they cook. Keep them in a cool cupboard in brown paper or cloth bags. There's also nothing like beautiful tomatoes

ripening in a lovely bowl, they don't behave well in a cold climate. If fruit flies descend on any ripe fruits before you have time to use them all then pop them in the fridge so they keep a little longer.

A little word about freezers

I personally struggle with freezers, which to many are essentially the black hole of the kitchen. You may never see those leftovers again or if you do months down the line you possibly wouldn't want to eat them anyway. I dislike the thought of eating cooked food that's been frozen for months unless it's edamame, peas or broad beans. Of course I must give these timeless storage keepers the credit they deserve for allowing easy access to my favourite pane pugliese

bread, those useful ice cubes, iced sherbets and the sort of support you need to cosset your inner slob. So if, like me, you can't eat a very small but deliciously meaty stew all in one go and you couldn't possibly eat the same thing again within the week then the freezer justifies its existence in a corner of your kitchen or utility room. Just don't make it the only way to eat, otherwise the pleasure of eating freshly cooked food may be lost forever along with the contents of that deep,

deep freezer. Remember: label and date all the things you stuff in there; if nothing else it will make you feel terribly self-righteous.

If time is precious and you don't want to shop more than once or twice in a week there are some things that are important to note. Naturally, make sure sell-by dates cover your use-by time slot. If you know you will be out a lot in a week, but still need a back up at home, choose ingredients that will last, such as lightly smoked salmon fillets, sausages, a fat chorizo, goat's cheese or a fillet steak to throw into a marinade to tenderise for days. With a back-up of prepared polenta or quinoa, some chard, tomatoes and courgettes you won't be short of a swift meal.

A word on kitchen equipment

If you have ever done a course in survival and you possess a sense of adventure you will know that you don't need much specialised equipment to feed yourself. But it helps back home to have your most useful and best-loved equipment which can be pivotal to making your solo task in the kitchen a pleasure and not a pain. It's all about your connection with your kitchen, so make it your own space with your favourite things around you.

My intention is not to give a long list of very specific utensils required, as unless new to cooking we just have what we have and over time discover the ones best suited to our own style of cooking. It goes without saying that a good range of sharp knives is as essential as a sturdy wooden chopping board. A set of pans, ranging from a dinky one small enough to reduce a few tablespoons of liquid through to a good chunky size to hold water at a full rolling boil for cooking pasta or simmering a chicken carcass into rich tasty stock, is a necessity.

Of course there are a few useful things to collect above and beyond the usual items most home cooks will have anyway. The major one for me is the very simple and eminently adaptable collapsible wire basket

steamer. It fits virtually any pan or wok you might have. Not specifically to only to steam vegetables and prawns but to reheat food without it tasting like yesterday's leftover dinner, even if it is! It performs miracles on mundane cold mash that tastes awful if not fried to golden brown nuggets. Steamed in an open bowl with a lid placed over the pan the mash is magically returned to its former glory.

Pick up useful tools such as sieves, colanders, slotted spoons, an oyster knife and lots and lots of bowls in junk and vintage shops. Enamel, heavy-based, lidded casseroles for slow cooking can often be foudn too, otherwise put on your birthday list. These items are all relatively cheap and always look like they have been loved and at the heart of an interesting kitchen or two.

A simple old-fashioned tin opener is very cheap and makes life easy. I have little patience, so trying to open a can with an all-singing all-dancing designer number – even though it's beautiful – makes me want to hit the gin. If you have an outdoor space, then a camping gas burner is the perfect thing for smoky steaks and sardines. Don't travel without one – great for beach trips.

It's essential to have a medium or large carbon

steel wok with a lid – they are cheap to buy in Asian supermarkets and, once seasoned, can be a lifetime's ally. Don't waste money on small or non-stick versions. Also a cast-iron frying pan is useful, not only because it's beautiful but because it's best for crunchy fried potatoes, as well as a non-stick version which can turn frying certain things from a trial to a pleasure. A ridged griddle pan for those steak moments, which can also be used outdoors on a barbecue or camping gas burner, is another useful addition.

A mini food processor with a wand blender attachment is handy for turning small quantities of anything into purée and for finely grinding nuts. Electric hand-held beaters are the most useful tool to get air into cakes. Build up a range of cake tins but you don't need many and neighbours will help out. A couple of sieves are always handy. Nylon ones are good for fruit as acid reacts with metal. For sifting flour and dry ingredients, a metal sieve will be ever-useful, but remember never put it in the dishwasher or it can rust.

Equipment doesn't have to be expensive and grand. I have made a Heath Robinson style egg prick to stop them bursting when hitting hot water. Take a wine bottle cork (perhaps having made good use of the contents of the bottle first) and stick a rounded dressmaker's pin through its equator so the round bit stops it going any further and the pointed end protrudes on the other side. Prick the round end of the egg where the air sac is and bursting eggs become a thing of the past.

Quick

Fixes

'Simplicity is the ultimate sophistication.'

Leonardo da Vinci

Seared halloumi with herb & saba dressing on tahini yogurt

Saba is undoubtedly my condiment of the moment, used as a sweetener and marinade since Roman times, it's a cooked, unfermented grape 'must' or juice with a deep, concentrated, raisin-like flavour. It pairs really well with soft cheeses, fruit and game, even ice cream. Also try Mugolio, a rich golden syrup made from the mugo pine cone bud that grows wild in the Italian Alps – it's my second favourite for use in this recipe.

6 green beans, stalk end trimmed, sliced in half lengthways

2–3 teaspoons lemon juice

1 tablespoon tahini

3 tablespoons natural yogurt or coconut yogurt

pinch sea salt crystals

2–3 x 1.5cm halloumi slices

½ teaspoon olive oil

2 teaspoons extra virgin olive oil, to serve

2 teaspoons saba or vincotta, to serve

a few sprigs of marjoram or oregano, leaves only

pinch of sumac, to dust

Cook the beans in a pan of salted boiling water for about 3 minutes until just cooked. Drain well, return to the pan and place the lid on. Set aside.

Mix the lemon juice, tahini, yogurt and salt together – check for taste and texture adding a little cold water to get a soft consistency, then spoon it onto a serving dish. Heat a non-stick frying pan over a high heat, coat the halloumi on both sides with the olive oil and sear for 1½–2 minutes or until golden. Reduce the heat a little and turn the pieces over to sear the other side.

Put the halloumi on top of the tahini yogurt, spoon over the extra virgin olive oil, dribble with the saba and sprinkle over the marjoram then dust with sumac. Lay the warm beans next to the halloumi.

WASTE NOT

Use any remaining halloumi and green beans for *Grilled halloumi, green beans, beetroot and mixed onion salad* (page 79).

Pear, watercress, beetroot & Gorgonzola salad with hazelnuts

Getting home late without much energy, you don't want a meal that's too heavy. This is a nice, neat little salad, which you could follow up with a tiny piece of cake and a few berries – definitely something worth coming home to.

about 25g or a couple of handfuls of watercress

1 large red, golden or candy beetroot, cooked

1 just-ripe red or Conference pear

75g Gorgonzola dolce

1 tablespoon *Mustard and white balsamic vinaigrette* (page 207)

1 tablespoon *Crispy capers* (page 202)

1 tablespoon *Smoky caramelised hazelnuts* (page 204), roughly chopped

Pop the watercress onto a plate, slice the beetroot and place it on top. Cut the pear in half, scoop out the core then slice thinly. Layer onto the plate and top with scoops of Gorgonzola dolce, spoon over the dressing and scatter over the capers and caramelised nuts.

Figs baked with honey & rose water

When figs are plentiful with beautiful deep red flesh, I like them baked; they turn soft and gooey inside. Serve them with a hint of indulgence – a slice of honeycomb and Vignotte, which is a lemony triple cream cheese from Normandy. Try to buy honeycomb in a jar, so it lasts for a while.

4 ripe figs

1 teaspoon honey

2 teaspoons rose water

honeycomb, to serve

Vignotte or Chaource, to serve

Preheat the oven to 220°C/gas mark 7.

Cut the figs in half lengthways and lay them cut-side up in a small ovenproof dish or pie tin. In a small bowl, mix the honey with the rose water and spoon it over the figs. Bake for 5–10 minutes until the figs are soft and oozing pink juices. Serve with the honeycomb and Vignotte.

WASTE NOT

You could also use figs in the *Pear, watercress, beetroot and Gorgonzola salad with hazelnuts* on page 20 instead of pears. The Vignotte can be used in *Toasted sourdough with Vignotte, curly kale and mushrooms* (page 32) or *Quick fix sweet treats* (page 69).

Wild garlic &
nettle vichyssoise

My spring medicine soup is perfect for the solo cook. It's easy to forage or grow a few leaves in the garden or allotment, nettle (*Urtica dioica*) never being a problem to find. Always check what you are picking is edible. Many good greengrocers and markets sell foraged wild garlic and nettles now. This soup is classically served cold but if you want, serve it hot, there are no rules.

a gloved handful of young nettle tops

20 broad-leaved wild garlic leaves

2 tablespoons olive oil

150g leeks, split, washed and roughly chopped

1 garlic clove, crushed with a little salt or 1 teaspoon *Crushed garlic* (page 207)

1 leftover cooked potato, cut into rough cubes

sea salt

125ml whipping cream

garlic flowers, to serve

Pour 750ml boiling water from the kettle into a medium pan and when it comes back to the boil add the nettles and cook for 30 seconds, then add the garlic leaves and cook for 20 seconds. Drain through a sieve set over a bowl to catch the cooking liquid, set aside the liquid and refresh the greens in a bowl of cold water and drain again.

Dry the pan and return to the heat and add the oil, leeks and crushed garlic and cook over a low heat for about 5 minutes until softened, not coloured. Increase the heat and add the potato, salt and the reserved liquid from blanching the nettles and the greens. When it comes to the boil, reduce the heat and cook for 8 minutes before stirring in 100ml of the cream. Pour into a bowl and cool it down quickly by placing the bowl in a larger bowl of cold water. Leave to cool.

Add the nettles and garlic leaves and process to a purée in a blender. Hand-whisk the remaining cream until just floppy. Ladle the soup into a bowl and swirl a little cream onto the top and scatter over some garlic flowers.

Things on toast

'So what did you eat when you got home?' is one of my FAQs and being a curious food obsessive I need and love to know these things. 'Oh, just a piece of toast', is the common reply. This section is for those people who know they should take toast a wee bit further even after a heavy day when they can't be moved to manage much more.

For a start, use bread that's worthy of you. There's perhaps a single occasion out there when sliced white is just the thing – Melba toast being its saving grace. So choose well – sourdough makes great toast, as does pane pugliese, the golden durum wheat bread made from the low-gluten flour of Altamura in southern Italy, which is also brilliant for chargrilling.

Sobrasada on toast with asparagus, crispy capers & a soft-boiled egg

Some people have a passion for sobrasada, a soft chorizo-style pâté made from cured pork of the Iberian pata negra pig. Many consider the fat to be 'good fat' due to the high oleic acid (a mono-unsaturated fatty acid) present in the acorns the pigs gorge on. Sobrasada is the extra virgin olive oil of the pig world: just make sure it's Iberico and organic. I like to keep a pack of sobrasada in the fridge to spread on toast for a meaty treat. If you can't manage to eat the whole pack within a few days, it does freeze well.

You can choose a brand from its spiritual home, Mallorca, or even 'Nduja – very similar but hotter – it's from Calabria in Italy and available from delis and some supermarkets. You could enjoy this with a handful of rocket or peppery watercress instead of asparagus.

125g untrimmed asparagus (or about half a bunch)

1–2 slices of sourdough bread or bread of choice

1 garlic clove, peeled

2 tablespoons extra virgin olive oil

40g sobrasada or 'Nduja

2 teaspoons olive oil

freshly ground black pepper

4 green tomatoes, quartered (optional)

1 large egg

1 tablespoon *Crispy capers* (page 202)

micro red vein sorrel leaves (optional), to serve

Trim the asparagus and put them in cold water; this helps to keep their fresh green colour. Get the extractor fan going and heat a ridged griddle pan over a high heat until just smoking. Griddle the bread for about 2 minutes until you have golden stripes on one side. Rub the griddled side of each slice of bread with the garlic clove, spoon over a little of the extra virgin olive oil and spread with the sobrasada.

Drain and dry the asparagus with kitchen paper, toss in half of the olive oil and grind over some pepper. Place on the griddle over a medium–high heat and cook for about 4 minutes, turning occasionally, until charred. Put the toast back on the griddle pan to lightly cook the underside, which will melt the sobrasada a little.

Meanwhile, heat a pan with the remaining olive oil and fry the green tomatoes for 4 minutes until just softened.

Fill a small saucepan with water and bring to the boil, cook the egg for 4 minutes. Drain.

Slice the asparagus in half lengthways and put them on top of the sobrasada then scatter over the capers and micro leaves (if using). Spoon over the remaining extra virgin olive oil and serve with the egg in a cup alongside.

Sardines on toast with tapenade, green tomatoes, celery & leaves

WASTE NOT

For more recipes with asparagus, see Lunchtime verrine on page 118 or serve with *Seared halloumi with herb and saba dressing on tahini yogurt* (page 18) instead of beans.

This is one of my favourite snack meals. Green tomatoes are delicious when tossed in a little vinaigrette and they also work well to cut through the richness of the sardines. But if you don't have them, use cucumber instead. It's worth making the *Tapenade* on page 200, which really does transform this into something special.

120g can best-quality sardines in olive oil

1 large slice of your favourite bread

2 tablespoons *Tapenade* (page 198)

1 teaspoon *Mustard and white balsamic vinaigrette* (page 207)

2 green tomatoes, sliced

1 celery stick, finely sliced, plus leaves to serve

1–2 pinches of cayenne pepper

Lift the sardines onto a plate, leaving the oil in the can. Toast or griddle the bread and spread over as much of the sardine oil as you like, followed by the tapenade.

Put the tomatoes and celery in a bowl and toss with the vinaigrette and arrange on the toast with sardines. Top with some celery leaves and cayenne pepper.

Goat's cheese, apple & spinach toasts with sumac & sesame salt

For me, this is the ultimate quick fix. Swap the toast for a few leftover potatoes that have been fried until crisp and golden (page 96) and serve with some steamed *Puy lentils* for a more filling meal (page 121).

1 pinky red-skinned apple

2 tablespoons olive oil

1–2 chunky slices of sourdough or bread of choice

100g goat's cheese with rind (about 4cm tall and 6cm in diameter)

80–100g baby spinach

small pinch of sea salt crystals

extra virgin olive oil, for serving

FOR THE SUMAC AND SESAME SALT

½ teaspoon sumac

½ teaspoon sesame seeds

1 teaspoon sea salt crystals

freshly ground black pepper

Preheat the grill to high and place the rack about 15cm away from the heat.

Cut the apple into quarters, remove the core then cut each piece into four. Heat 1 tablespoon of the olive oil in a frying pan. Add the apple pieces and fry on both sides for about 8 minutes or until soft and just beginning to colour.

Mix the ingredients for the sumac and sesame salt together. Toast the bread on both sides and drizzle with a little of the extra virgin oil, then cover with foil to keep warm.

Meanwhile, line a small baking tray with foil. Cut the cheese in half horizontally and place it, cut-side up, on the tray and pour over a little olive oil and a few grindings of black pepper. Grill for 4 minutes or until golden and starting to bubble.

Put the spinach into a large bowl with the salt and pour over just-boiled water from the kettle to cover. Leave for a minute until just wilted, drain well and stir in the remaining olive oil.

Pile the spinach and apple onto the toast and top with the soft grilled cheese. To serve, spoon over the extra virgin olive oil, scatter with sumac and sesame salt and eat straightaway.

Toasted sourdough with Vignotte, curly kale & mushrooms

Buy a piece of Vignotte just to have in the fridge as it's so good with fruit or as a dessert with the *Elderberry jelly* on page 185. It's a cow's milk cheese from Normandy with a creamy, super-rich, buttery texture. Chaource would make a good substitute. You could use any assortment of mushrooms. Maybe you have a few shimeji to use up after making the *Pea and lemon risotto* on page 172. To prepare the kale, strip the leaves and discard the tough stalks.

2 tablespoons olive oil

90g chestnut mushrooms, sliced

1 Portobello or large flat mushroom, sliced

1 garlic clove, crushed to a paste with a little salt or 1 teaspoon *Crushed garlic* (page 207)

1 slice of sourdough bread

splash of extra virgin olive oil, plus extra to serve

2 handfuls of prepared curly kale leaves or baby spinach

2–3 slices of Vignotte

truffle oil or extra virgin olive oil, to serve

sea salt crystals and freshly ground black pepper

Heat half the olive oil in a large frying pan and add the sliced mushrooms, let them sear on one side for a minute or so before moving them. Continue to cook down for a few minutes until there is no liquid in the pan. Stir in half the garlic and cook for a minute then lightly season with salt and pepper.

Meanwhile, toast or griddle the sourdough on both sides, transfer to a plate then add the splash of extra virgin olive oil to moisten the toast.

Heat the remaining olive oil in a wok over a low heat, add the remaining garlic and when it sizzles add the kale, cover and cook for 4 minutes.

Preheat the grill to high and set the rack about 15cm from the heat.

Pile the kale onto the toast followed by the cooked mushrooms. Put the Vignotte slices on top and pop under the grill for a minute to lightly melt. Grind over some black pepper and pour over a little truffle oil and/or extra virgin olive oil to finish.

Charred ciabatta with smoky steak, courgettes & aubergine

Espelette pepper is from the Basque region of France bordering with Spain. It's a finely ground, fragrantly fruity yet piquant chilli pepper with undertones of saltiness and the seeds are usually removed after drying. Use the aubergine cooked in *Hünkar beğendi* (page 136) for this recipe or slice and cook a small aubergine in the same way as the courgette. If you have a few cherry tomatoes, halve them and throw under the grill with the courgettes for the last 3 minutes of grilling and serve with some vinaigrette-dressed rocket or other salad leaves.

1 x 100g thick piece of fillet steak

4 teaspoons olive oil

1 garlic clove, crushed with a little salt or 1 teaspoon *Crushed garlic* (page 207)

200g courgette, sliced

½ teaspoon Espelette pepper or crushed chilli flakes

extra virgin olive oil, to serve

1 thick slice of ciabatta, halved horizontally

1 portion of *Hünkar beğendi* (page 136) or 1 small aubergine, sliced

sea salt crystals and freshly ground black pepper

Preheat the grill to high and set the rack about 15cm from the heat.

Put the fillet steak in a dish with 2 teaspoons of the olive oil, the garlic and black pepper. Leave to marinate while you prepare the other ingredients.

Line a baking tray with foil and add the courgette slices, toss with 2 teaspoons of olive oil and spread them out in a single layer. Sprinkle over the Espelette pepper and grill for about 10 minutes, turning halfway through for perfect lightly charred pieces. Transfer to a bowl and dress with a little extra virgin olive oil.

Meanwhile, heat a ridged griddle pan over a high heat and griddle the bread, cut-side down. Spoon over a little extra virgin olive oil for serving and keep warm. Ensure the griddle pan is smoking hot, season the steak with a little salt on both sides then add to the pan and cook for 1½ minutes on each side for rare or about 2 minutes for medium rare. Leave to rest until the other ingredients are ready.

Pile some courgettes and Hünkar beğendi onto the ciabatta and slice the steak and put on top. Spoon over some more extra virgin olive oil and serve.

Salad lyonnaise

There always seems to be lettuce and smoky bacon lardons in the fridge, some bread around and an egg to use up. This classic warm salad is a great vehicle to use up all the bits. Bring them all together with the *Mustard and white balsamic vinaigrette* on page 207. It also makes a great supper; instead of turning the bread into croutons, you could toast it, rub it with garlic and drench in peppery extra virgin olive oil.

some frisée, Little Gem or escarole lettuce (or any you have)

2 tablespoons olive oil

60g smoked bacon lardons

1 slice good-quality bread, cubed

1 tablespoon *Mustard and white balsamic vinaigrette* (page 207)

1 hen or duck egg

sea salt crystals and freshly ground black pepper

Separate the lettuce leaves and arrange in a bowl. Heat 1 teaspoon of the oil in a frying pan over a medium heat and fry the lardons until just golden. Tip onto a plate lined with kitchen paper and give the pan a wipe.

Heat the remaining oil until hot then add the bread and fry until golden and crunchy.

Dress the salad and scatter over the lardons and croutons.

Bring a pan of salted water to the boil. Break the egg into a cup and use a spoon to swirl the water, gently slip the egg into the vortex, reduce the heat and poach for about 2 minutes or until the white is set around the yolk. Use a slotted spoon to lift the egg onto the salad and scatter with salt and freshly ground black pepper.

WASTE NOT

If you have a ripe avocado half, add spoonfuls of the flesh over this salad too.

My quick-fix breakfast of buttered egg with crispy crumbs

This quick breakfast is perfect with some fried bacon or pancetta chopped up into the breadcrumbs along with some parsley leaves. If you make *Marinated herb-crusted rack of lamb* on page 173, prepare extra crumbs and keep for the morning after. Pul biber pepper flakes (also known as Aleppo pepper) hails from Turkey and Syria. The coarsely ground capsicum flakes are renowned for their mild, sweet, warm flavour with undertones of saltiness: I'm hooked.

2 tablespoons olive oil

3 rashers of smoked streaky bacon or thin pancetta, finely chopped

1 small slice of good-quality bread, crusts removed and finely chopped, or put in a mini food processor and whizzed to a crumb

a few stems of parsley, leaves removed and chopped

1 duck or hen egg

30g butter

½ teaspoon *Toasted sesame seeds* (page 200)

a few pinches of pul biber pepper or chilli flakes

sea salt crystals

pinch of sumac, to scatter

Heat the oil in a frying pan over a medium–high heat and fry the bacon for 1 minute. Add the breadcrumbs and continue to fry for a further minute then add the parsley and cook for about 2 minutes, until crisp and golden.

Break the egg into a small glass. Melt the butter in a small saucepan over a medium heat and tilt the pan so the butter gathers in a puddle on one side then lower the heat. Gently pour the egg into the butter and add a pinch of salt. Fry for about 2 minutes until cooked. Use a slotted spoon to lift the egg out onto a serving plate lined with kitchen paper, leaving the egg to drain in the spoon.

Put the sesame seeds and pul biber into the hot crumbs and reheat. Lift the egg off the plate, remove the kitchen paper (you now have a warm plate), add the crumbs, top with the egg and scatter with sumac.

Avocado, quail egg & brown shrimp salad with wasabi soy dressing

Brown shrimp have that salty taste of the sea and can be picked up from the fishmonger, who usually carries the quail eggs too, otherwise a good supermarket will have all you need. You could even use samphire instead of salad – just blanch it for a few minutes in boiling water. If you want a more substantial dish, take a portion of cooked *Quinoa* (page 130), fold a few nuts and seeds through and serve it along with this combination of lovely flavours.

4 quail eggs

½ large ripe avocado

50g prepared brown shrimp (about ½ pack)

a big handful of peppery salad leaves, such as rocket or watercress

FOR THE WASABI SOY DRESSING

¼ teaspoon wasabi paste

1½ teaspoons light soy sauce

1 tablespoon olive oil

First, make the dressing. Put the wasabi paste in a small bowl, mix in the soy sauce, a little at a time, then whisk in the oil. Set aside.

Fill a small saucepan with water and bring to the boil. Lower the eggs into the pan and cook for 1 minute. Remove from the heat and set aside for a further minute to cool.

Put the avocado half on a plate and pile on the brown shrimp. Place the salad leaves alongside and spoon some wasabi soy dressing over everything. Peel the quail eggs very gently as they are still soft inside and put them on top of the salad to finish.

WASTE NOT

You only need half a pack of brown shrimp for the recipe above – this will use up the remainder. Heat a few knobs of butter in a small pan, add the shrimp, a grinding of nutmeg and a squeeze of lemon juice. Transfer to a small pot and chill when completely cold. Serve with toast.

Allotment leaf & flower salad with goat's cheese & elderflower dressing

If you grow salad and herb leaves and edible flowers in pots on a balcony, garden or allotment, just pick a few leaves and flowers as and when you want to make this salad. You can also buy a few handfuls of an array of salad and herbs from farmers' markets – what you are after is a good variety of leaves.

a mixed assortment of leaves, such as wild or broadleaf rocket, buckler leaf sorrel, fennel fronds, baby beetroot or baby chard leaves, salad burnet, nasturtium leaves, mizuna, marjoram, nasturtium leaves and flowers, viola or pansy flowers, small lettuce leaves

60g soft goat's cheese, goat's curd or Vignotte

FOR THE ELDERFLOWER DRESSING

1 tablespoon *Elderflower cordial* (page 182) or juice of ½ lemon

2 tablespoons olive oil

1 tablespoon extra virgin olive oil

pinch of sea salt crystals

As soon as you pick the leaves, sort them and put in cold water for 5 minutes. Rinse the flowers and put between kitchen paper in a box in the fridge. Drain the leaves and store in the same way in a separate box.

When ready to eat, make the dressing by putting all the ingredients in a jar with a secure screw-top lid, tighten it and shake vigorously to emulsify.

Put the leaves and flowers in a bowl and toss with as much of the dressing as you want. Scoop pieces of the soft goat's cheese or curd over the salad and eat. Any leftover dressing will keep in the fridge for up to 4 days.

WASTE NOT

Put leaves and flowers between 2 slices of thickly buttered bread and cut into squares to eat at teatime.

Chicken with
Marsala & sage

If you have saved a leg of chicken in oil and frozen it from *My perfect roast chicken* (page 176), get it out on the morning you want to prepare this recipe for supper. Otherwise buy a large chicken leg from the butcher. They will happily remove the skin and cut it into pieces for you if you ask them with a smile. Remember to ask for the bones – you can use them in stock (see page 179).

2 teaspoons olive oil

3 rashers of smoked streaky bacon, sliced into thin strips

15g salted butter

1 large leg or 2 large chicken thighs, skinned, boned and cut into 1 cm pieces

5 sage leaves

4 tablespoons Marsala

Heat 1 teaspoon of the olive oil in a frying pan over a medium heat and fry the bacon for about 3 minutes until golden. Transfer onto a plate with a slotted spoon and wipe the pan clean with kitchen paper.

Heat the remaining oil and the butter over a medium heat and fry the chicken and sage for 2 minutes. Add 2 tablespoons of the Marsala, letting it boil down with the chicken before adding the rest. Cook for a further 2 minutes making sure the chicken is cooked and the Marsala has evaporated. Serve with some pasta rags from the freezer (see page 63; no need to defrost before cooking) or some shop-bought pasta if wished and some steamed purple sprouting broccoli or romanesco.

Black pudding, caramelised persimmon & freekeh with raspberry salad cream

I'm a great fan of a good, traditional Irish additive-free black pudding, packed with pinhead oatmeal without a lot of fatty bits. I also sometimes like to use morcilla as it gives me an excuse to visit my favourite Spanish shop where I often come out inspired to cook many a good dish. If you love haggis (including vegetarian haggis) you could easily use that instead.

4 tablespoons olive oil

2 teaspoons *Raspberry vinegar* (page 213) or shop-bought raspberry vinegar

1 teaspoon good-quality mayonnaise

1 ripe but firm persimmon or Cox's apple

2 teaspoons caster sugar

1 small banana shallot, finely chopped

1 garlic clove, crushed to a paste with a little salt or 1 teaspoon *Crushed garlic* (page 207)

⅓–½ portion of *Freekeh* (page 130)

4 rashers of pancetta

1 x 100g piece of black pudding with oatmeal or morcilla, skin removed and roughly sliced

toasted sesame, sunflower and pumpkin seeds, to scatter

a handful of baby spinach leaves

a handful of baby red chard leaves

grissini, to serve

First make the raspberry salad cream. Pour 2 tablespoons of olive oil, the raspberry vinegar and mayonnaise into a jar with a screw-top jar with a secure lid and shake vigorously to emulsify.

Pull the hard top off the persimmon, cut into quarters and cut each piece into three wedges. Heat the sugar and the fruit in a frying pan over a medium–low heat and let them caramelise gently for a few minutes on each side. Carefully lift out onto a plate, set aside and give the pan a wipe.

Heat 1 tablespoon of the oil in the pan over a medium heat, add the shallot and garlic and fry for about 5 minutes until soft then add the freekeh. Tip onto a warm plate.

Preheat the grill to high. Line a baking tray with foil and add the pancetta. Grill on both sides until just crispy. Remove onto a plate lined with kitchen paper to cool then roughly chop into shards.

Add the remaining oil to the pan along with the black pudding and fry over a medium–high heat for a few minutes until just crispy around the edges. Add some freekeh onto a serving plate, scatter over the toasted seeds, top with the crisp pancetta and black pudding, add the leaves and persimmon and spoon over the dressing. Serve with grissini.

Crispy sausage, red rice, romanesco & pomegranate

With such a huge variety of top-quality sausages now available it's possible to get real flavour into a dish without a long list of ingredients. The sausages liberated from their skins cook so much faster. I like to have a batch of red rice already made in advance (see *Red rice with saba*, page 121) and *Toasted pine nuts* ready from the shelf (page 200).

1 small romanesco or broccoli, separated into florets

2 tablespoons olive oil

2 x good-quality flavoursome fat sausages of choice, skin removed

2 sprigs parsley with a bit of stalk

½ portion cooked *Red rice* (page 121)

a scattering of *Toasted pine nuts* (page 200)

seeds from a piece of pomegranate

saba or vincotto, to serve

Cook the romanesco florets in a pan of boiling salted water for about 4 minutes or until cooked to your liking. Drain and refresh under cold water and drain again. This will stop them from cooking and keep them bright green.

Heat 1 tablespoon of the oil in a large frying pan over a high heat and crumble in the skinned sausage meat. Use a fork to break it up as it fries and keep it moving around so it doesn't stick as it breaks up into crumbs. Add the remaining oil, frying the meat until cooked through and golden brown.

Using kitchen scissors, roughly snip the parsley straight into the pan. Stir in the red rice and cooked romanesco to heat through. Scatter with pine nuts and pomegranate seeds, trickle over some saba and serve.

Smoked trout pâté

I tried using wasabi instead of horseradish as I didn't have any in the fridge along with lime juice instead of lemon and it really worked. You can also use pure coconut yogurt instead of cream cheese.

As the recipe makes enough for two servings, eat the second serving of pâté a few days later for a quick supper with a scooped out avocado, slices of cooked beetroot or *Beetroot crane* (page 136) along with some salad leaves dressed with vinaigrette (page 207).

MAKES ENOUGH FOR 2 PORTIONS

80g full-fat soft cream cheese

1½ teaspoons wasabi paste or
    2½ teaspoons horseradish sauce

juice of ½ lime or lemon

75g hot-smoked trout fillet

a few fronds of dill

thin crispbreads or toast, to serve

Put the cream cheese in a bowl and mix in the wasabi and lime juice. Flake the trout into the mixture and use a fork to break it up into your desired texture. Chop the dill and mix it into the pâté. Eat straightaway or cover and store in the fridge for up to three days.

WASTE NOT

If you have any smoked trout remaining, use it in the *Bhuna khichuri* (page 154) instead of prawns or *Smoked trout with black rice noodles, broccoli and Asian pesto* (page 111).

Seared scallops & cauliflower crumbs with garlic, chilli & herb butter

I have developed a new fondness for cauliflower – there is always plenty left for a few more dishes when you buy a medium-sized fresh and creamy specimen.

All you need for this dish are the florets (or curds as they are known) and small pale leaves. The stems can be kept for another meal (see Waste not opposite).

2 x diver-caught scallops with or without roe, cleaned

2 tablespoons olive oil

100g cauliflower, broken into florets, stems removed and small leaves reserved

1 garlic clove, finely chopped

½ large red chilli, deseeded and finely chopped

1 teaspoon soft unsalted butter

a few sprigs of parsley, chopped

20g toasted hazelnuts, roughly crunched with the back of a heavy knife

sea salt crystals and freshly ground black pepper

Put the scallops on a plate, pour over 1 teaspoon of the oil, season and toss. Chop the cauliflower roughly – small and medium pieces are fine – then process a few bits in a mini food processor to a rough crumb. (This is to make it look nice so it's up to you how crumbly you like it.)

Heat 1 tablespoon of the oil in a wide frying pan, add the cauliflower crumbs in a single layer and fry until golden brown.

Meanwhile, in a bowl, mix the garlic and chilli with the butter and add it to the cauliflower along with the parsley and hazelnuts then season with salt and pepper. Tip into a bowl and use kitchen paper to wipe the pan.

Increase the heat and when the pan is nice and hot, add the scallops and sear for about 2 minutes on each side until golden (less time if the scallops are small). Put as much of the cauliflower mixture as you like on a plate and place the scallops on top. Wipe the pan again and heat the remaining 2 teaspoons of oil and any small pale leaves from the cauliflower and let them colour a little then remove and add to the plate.

WASTE NOT

To use the cauliflower stems, thinly slice them and squeeze over some lime juice and serve with any of the exciting salt combinations on page 208.

To use any excess cauliflower florets, make a purée. Blanch the florets, drain and add to a mini food processor with a small cooked potato, a little warmed cream and hot water and blitz until very soft.

Cauliflower can also be used in the *Roasted cauliflower, fennel and chorizo puchero* (page 93).

Or chop the florets and stir-fry in a wok with a dash of oil until golden, add 1 teaspoon of crushed garlic, ½ chopped chilli, a little grated fresh ginger, a pinch each of nigella seeds, crushed cumin and seasoning. Add 2 tablespoons of water, cover and cook for a few minutes until al dente.

Rope-grown mussels with garlic, tomato & loads of parsley

If you buy rope-grown mussels they won't need endless prep, as they are already very clean, just steep for 10 minutes in cold water to close them up. Then debeard them, discarding any that remain open. Cheat with a bowl of shop-bought thin oven chips to go with the mussels or serve with the *Shaved potato crisps* on page 215. It's handy to have washed your parsley after buying it, then pop the bunch into a jug of water until the leaves drip dry. Transfer to a box with damp kitchen paper, cover and store in the fridge.

300g rope-grown mussels, debearded

2 tablespoons olive oil

1 large banana shallot, finely chopped

2 garlic cloves, finely chopped

1 small or ½ large fennel bulb, finely chopped

1 celery stick and leaves, finely chopped

1 large tomato, skinned, deseeded and finely chopped (page 127)

1 wine glass of rosé or white wine

15g flat-leaf parsley, most of the stems discarded and leaves roughly chopped

Rinse the mussels in a colander under cold running water.

Heat the olive oil in a large pan over a medium-low heat and add the garlic, shallot, fennel and celery. Gently fry for about 5 minutes until soft and light golden in colour.

Increase the heat, add the tomato, stir, then add the wine and bubble for a few minutes, then add half the parsley.

Put the mussels into the pan, cover and cook for about 4 minutes, shaking the pan a little until the mussels open. Discard any that don't open. Add the remaining parsley and serve hot with a bowl of oven-cooked chips or *Shaved potato crisps* (page 215).

Squid vinaigrette

This is one of those meals that is great to eat right away but you can make ahead as it will keep happily in the fridge for up to two days. The amount of squid you will need will depend on size. Small- to medium-sized squid are best, and do buy from a fishmonger who will clean them for you. Cleaning them yourself is an easy, fun thing to do, and once learnt never forgotten.

about 400g squid with tentacles, cleaned

1 tablespoon olive oil

juice of ½ lemon

1 tablespoon *Mustard and white balsamic vinaigrette* (page 207)

3 sprigs of flat-leaf parsley, finely chopped

sea salt crystals and freshly ground black pepper

rocket, mizuna or other salad leaves of choice, to serve

Preheat the grill to medium and arrange the rack about 15cm from the heat. Cut each squid across into 2–3 even-sized pieces. Line a baking tray with foil and place the squid and tentacles on top. Add the oil, lemon juice and season with salt and pepper and toss to coat.

Grill the squid pieces for 3–4 minutes on each side. Transfer to a small dish, along with the juices from the baking tray and immediately pour over the mustard vinaigrette, turning them in the mixture. Eat warm or cover the dish once cooled and store in the fridge until 15 minutes before serving with a few leaves.

Grilled trout fillets, baby leeks & toasted pine nuts with romesco sauce

Simplicity is key to this meal with a Spanish vibe. Make the romesco with all those bits and pieces from Those Little Extras chapter while the leeks and fish are under the grill.

175g baby leeks or 5 small leeks

2 teaspoons white balsamic vinegar

1½ tablespoons olive oil

1 x trout, filleted or 2 x prepared trout fillets

sea salt crystals and freshly ground black pepper

FOR THE ROMESCO SAUCE

1 medium tomato, peeled, deseeded and roughly chopped (see page 127)

1 x *Grilled marinated pepper* (page 200) or shop-bought marinated pepper

1 garlic clove, chopped

1 tablespoon *Toasted pine nuts* (page 200), plus extra to serve

1 tablespoon red wine vinegar

½ teaspoon smoked paprika

4 pinches of pul biber pepper flakes

100ml extra virgin olive oil

To make the romesco sauce, put everything except half the oil into a mini processor and blend until smooth. Add the remaining oil in two batches and blend again until you have a thick sauce.

Preheat the grill to high and arrange the rack about 15cm from the heat. Line a baking tray with foil.

Slit the leeks lengthways, leaving most of the root tip on – don't cut all the way through – and wash well. Lay them on the prepared tray, season and add the white balsamic vinegar and 1 tablespoon of the oil.

Grill for 6–8 minutes turning halfway through the cooking time. Transfer to a plate, wrapped in the foil from the baking tray. Cover the tray with another piece of foil, season the trout on both sides and spoon over the remaining oil. Grill skin-side up for about 5 minutes until blistered and cooked through (the flesh should be opaque).

Arrange the leeks on a serving plate with the fish and scatter with the extra pine nuts. Put some of the romesco in a small bowl to serve.

WASTE NOT

Any remaining romesco sauce could be used with some grilled asparagus or with the *Tray-roasted vegetables* on page 89 instead of salsa salmoriglio.

Pak choi, chilli & ginger with baked fish

I like to buy really spanking fresh fish, the idea being that half is eaten fresh and the remainder can be salted a day or two before I plan to cook it, so it does for a few meals. Sprinkle with a little salt on the flesh side, and put uncovered in the fridge. However, if you haven't salted the fish and you are using a just-bought fresh piece, this dish will still be delicious. Use sliced spring onions and courgettes too if you have them, along with any coriander leaves left on a bunch in the fridge. If you have it to hand a portion of cooked black rice (see page 121) folded through looks beautiful with the pure white fish.

1 x 200g cod fillet, skin on

2 teaspoons olive oil

200g pak choi

1 tablespoon sunflower oil

1 red chilli, deseeded and finely chopped

2cm finger-thick piece of fresh ginger, peeled and grated

1 garlic clove, finely sliced

1 tablespoon light soy sauce

1 teaspoon toasted sesame oil

sea salt crystals and freshly ground black pepper

Preheat the oven to 190°C/gas mark 5. Line a small oven tray with foil. If you have salted the fish a day or two before, then wash it off, pat dry with kitchen paper and season with pepper. If not, season the fish with salt and pepper. Place it on the prepared tray flesh side up and spoon over the olive oil. Cook for 9–11 minutes, depending on the thickness. When done, the flesh will be opaque and flake easily. (Remove skin when serving.)

Meanwhile, trim the pak choi and slice it into 3cm pieces, wash in a colander and set aside to drain.

Heat a wok over a medium heat, add the sunflower oil and stir-fry the chilli, ginger and garlic for 30 seconds. Add the pak choi and stir-fry for a few seconds more then add the soy sauce, cover and reduce the heat to low to cook for a further 2 minutes. Stir in the sesame oil and serve with the cod.

Borlotti, tuna & herbs with grilled artichokes, cherry tomatoes & grissini

When in season, I prefer fresh borlotti rather than the canned variety, not only for their beautiful pink speckled hue but also for their ability to be cooked in minutes. If you are lucky enough to grow your own – even better.

120g can line-caught tuna steak in extra virgin olive oil

3 artichoke hearts from a can or jar, drained and halved lengthways

a small bunch of cherry tomatoes on the vine

a few handfuls of fresh borlotti beans or 1 can of borlotti beans or butterbeans, drained and rinsed well

a handful of flat-leaf parsley, leaves chopped

a few sprigs marjoram or oregano, leaves only, chopped

1 tablespoon *Mustard and white balsamic vinaigrette* (page 207)

grissini, to serve

Drain the tuna, reserving the oil.

Preheat the grill to high and set the rack about 15cm from the heat. Line a baking tray with foil and place the artichokes cut-side up on the tray. Spoon over a little of the reserved tuna oil. Arrange the tomatoes on the tray and place under the grill until the artichokes are golden and the tomatoes are just splitting.

If using fresh beans, boil in salted water for 5 minutes until tender. Put the beans in a bowl, add the herbs and pour in the vinaigrette then flake over the tuna, turning it into the mixture. Serve with the artichokes and tomatoes and grissini.

Cod fillet with rainbow chard & sobrasada

This works particularly well served with either the Red rice with saba (page 121), or you could crisply fry some new potato slices in olive oil as an accompaniment.

When cooking with fish, I like to buy double the amount – one piece to eat right away and one to use later on in the week. I simply sprinkle the extra fillet with a little sea salt on the flesh side, cover and chill. It will keep for two days like this and can be used in *Pak choi, chilli and ginger with baked fish* (page 56) or *Goan fish curry* (page 107).

1 x 200g piece cod or pollock fillet, skin on

1½ tablespoons olive oil

6 large leaves rainbow or Swiss chard

40g piece sobrasada or 'Nduja (see page 28), skin removed

sea salt crystals and freshly ground black pepper

Preheat the oven to 200°C/gas mark 6. Line a small oven tray with foil and add the cod, flesh side up. Add a pinch of salt and a grinding of black pepper to the flesh and spoon over ½ tablespoon of oil. Set aside while you prepare the chard.

Strip the chard leaves off their stems and tear into large chunks then slice the stems into 1cm pieces. Put the stems and the remaining oil in a large wok set over a medium–high heat and stir-fry for about 2 minutes until the stems soften a little. Remove from the heat, add the leaves along with 50ml water, return to the heat and wilt the leaves for about 3 minutes or until just tender. Drain through a sieve, return to the pan and cover.

Meanwhile, place the fish in the oven and cook for about 9 minutes, depending on thickness. Just before it's ready put the chard back over a medium heat and crumble in the sobrasada, stirring to break it up and to heat it through. Serve immediately with the cod skin removed as you serve.

WASTE NOT

You can use any leftover sobrasada for *Sobrasada on toast with asparagus, crispy capers and a soft-boiled egg* (page 28).

Crab & herb omelette tagliatelle with samphire salad

This salad simply involves a quick trip to the fishmonger for the samphire and crabmeat. Together with bits and pieces from the fridge and larder, you'll have a meal in minutes that is unbelievably tasty. Buy dulse in healthfood shops or online.

a few pieces of dulse (a dried sea vegetable) or sea vegetable salad

50g young samphire, hard stems removed

3cm piece cucumber (Lebanese, if available)

4 radishes

2 large eggs

1 garlic clove, crushed to a paste with a little salt or 1 teaspoon *Crushed garlic* (page 207)

¼ teaspoon sesame oil

½ teaspoon light soy sauce

a handful of coriander leaves

50–60g white crabmeat

1 teaspoon sunflower oil

pinch of pul biber pepper flakes

FOR THE DRESSING

1 teaspoon light soy sauce

2 teaspoons white balsamic vinegar

¼ teaspoon sesame oil

large pinch of coconut palm sugar

First, make the dressing. Put the ingredients into a small bowl, whisk with a fork and set aside.

Rinse the dulse well and soak in cold water for a few minutes to soften. Tear into strips and transfer to a bowl. Bring a small pan of water to the boil and blanch the samphire for 30 seconds–1 minute until just tender. Drain and refresh under cold water. Drain again and pat dry with kitchen paper and add to the dulse.

Thinly slice the cucumber and the radishes lengthways and then into matchsticks. Add them to the dulse and samphire then fold in the dressing.

Break the eggs into a bowl and whisk in ½ tablespoon of water. Add the garlic, sesame oil and soy sauce. Chop the coriander and add with all but 1 tablespoon of the crabmeat and fold to combine. Heat a 20cm frying pan over a medium–high heat, add half the oil and use kitchen paper to distribute it around in the inside of the pan. Reduce the heat and ladle in half the egg mixture, swirling to evenly cover the base of the pan. Let the mixture gently set and lightly colour for about 2 minutes. When you can turn it easily, flip it over and cook the other side for about a minute.

Remove from the heat and ease the omelette onto a chopping board, roll into a cigar shape and set aside. Repeat with the remaining mixture and slice the omelettes into pieces, about 0.7mm wide (the thickness of tagliatelle). Tip onto a serving plate, add the remaining crabmeat to the samphire salad and add to the plate. Scatter over the pul biber.

WASTE NOT

If you have bought extra samphire in a pack, use any left over within two days along with any remaining crabmeat in *Crab, courgette and maftoul salad* (page 112).

Pasta rags
with mackerel

Pasta con le sarde, a Sicilian dish, is the inspiration for this recipe. Although sardines are traditionally used, I find that mackerel are a more convenient option for picking up on the way home. If herrings or sardines are in season, and in perfect condition, by all means use them. I've swapped bucatini, the long, fat pasta with a hole down the centre, for 'rags' torn from homemade pasta sheets (see page 120) but you can also tear shop-bought fresh lasagne sheets or use pappardelle instead. It's a good idea to keep any rags of fresh pasta in the freezer so they can easily be cooked from frozen if you intend using them for this dish.

20g raisins

30g crusty white bread of choice (pane pugliese – golden durum wheat bread – is good)

pinch of ground cinnamon

pinch of cayenne pepper

grating of nutmeg

3 tablespoons olive oil

100g red or white onion, thinly sliced then roughly chopped

100g fennel bulb, very thinly sliced lengthways

2 mackerel fillets, skin on

25g pistachio nibs or whole, skinned nuts, chopped

about 50g pasta rags (page 120), shop-bought lasagne, torn, or pappardelle

sea salt crystals and freshly ground black pepper

extra virgin olive oil, to serve

pinch of fennel pollen (optional), to serve

Soak the raisins in a bowl of cold water while you prepare the remaining ingredients. Blitz the bread in a mini food processor, until you have chunky crumbs. Mix in the cinnamon, cayenne, nutmeg and a little salt. Heat 1 tablespoon of the olive oil in a frying pan and fry the crumbs until golden and crispy, then tip into a small bowl and set aside.

Wipe out the pan, heat the remaining olive oil over a medium heat and fry the onion for about 2 minutes. Add the fennel and continue to cook until the onion is golden, about 3 minutes. Push the mix to one side of the pan and add the mackerel, skin-side down, until the flesh has become pale in colour and is no longer pink. Season with salt and pepper and remove to a plate lined with kitchen paper to drain. Add the drained raisins and pistachios to the pan, stirring into the fennel mixture to heat through.

Meanwhile, cook the homemade pasta in boiling salted water for 3–4 minutes or follow the packet instructions for shop-bought varieties. Drain and add to the pan along with the mackerel, letting it break up a litte into chunky pieces. Gently fold together and serve scattered with crispy crumbs, some extra virgin olive oil and a pinch of fennel pollen if you wish.

Ali's quick fix of ravioli, courgette & goat's cheese

This is Ali's, the wonderful photographer of *Solo*, favourite dish. It also works with spinach in place of the shaved courgettes. You could toss through any leftover broccoli mixture from *Lunchtime verrine* (page 118) or *Tarragon and hazelnut pesto* (page 201) if you wish.

125g good-quality pumpkin-stuffed ravioli or filled pasta of choice

1–2 courgettes, about 175g, (in green and yellow if available), shaved with a vegetable peeler into ribbons

4 teaspoons soft goat's cheese

extra virgin olive oil, to serve

freshly ground black pepper or *Dukka* mix (page 208), to serve

pinch of pul biber pepper flakes, to serve

Bring a pan of salted water to the boil and add the pasta. Cook for 5 minutes (don't over-boil them as they tend to split) or according to the packet instructions. When they are just about done, add the courgette ribbons for the last 20 seconds. Drain and put in a warmed bowl, dot with the spoons of goat's cheese, add a good slick of extra virgin olive oil, some pepper or dukka and the pinch of pul biber. Eat while hot.

Apricot & blueberry verrine with honeysuckle blossom

A verrine is a great way to serve an individual dessert; as the French name implies the ingredients are layered up in a glass. I sometimes double the amount of apricots here, as once cooked they will keep for a couple of days in the fridge and can be enjoyed with a bowl of porridge or used instead of the greengages for the *Eve's pudding* (page 159).

Coconut yogurt can be found in wholefood and health stores. Make sure you buy the pure thick, creamy variety not a dairy yogurt flavoured with coconut.

I small glass dry white wine, such as Pinot Grigio

2 tablespoons caster sugar, plus I teaspoon

I teaspoon vanilla bean paste

300g apricots, halved and stoned (about 6 apricots)

50g blueberries

2 amaretti morbidi (the soft sort, very useful to have in your cupboard), roughly crumbed

3 tablespoons coconut yogurt

a few scented honeysuckle petals, for a decorative flourish (*Lonicera japonica* flowers are edible; the berries not – optional)

Select a saucepan large enough to fit the apricots in a single layer, add the wine, sugar and vanilla bean paste and bring to a simmer.

Add the apricots and cover with a cartouche (a circle of baking parchment cut to the size of the saucepan) and lay it on top of the apricots then cover with a lid. Simmer gently for about 5 minutes or until the apricots are just soft then use a slotted spoon to transfer them to a bowl. Increase the heat and cook to reduce the liquid until you have a syrup. Now pour the syrup over the apricots, leaving about a tablespoon in the pan. Add the blueberries to the pan and cook for a few minutes until glossy. Remove from the heat and set aside to cool completely.

Make up your verrine by layering the ingredients prettily in a glass. Start with some apricots in the base, a little of the amaretti crumbs, some blueberries then the yogurt. Repeat the layering and finish with a dollop of yogurt on the top. Add a flourish of nectar-laden edible honeysuckle if available.

QUICK FIX SWEET TREATS

Sometimes we yearn for total indulgence, other times just something that can pass as a dessert and add that satisfying finish to a meal. These swift treats do the job perfectly.

Nectarine, passion fruit syrup & coconut yogurt

Put half a tub of coconut yogurt (not the dairy sort flavoured with coconut but the pure creamy sort) in a bowl. Spoon over the flesh from 1 scooped-out passion fruit, slice in a ripe nectarine and add a splash of that fragrant *Elderflower cordial* that you have sitting in the fridge (page 182). You could make a syrup (or use maple syrup for a sweeter hit) by putting another scooped-out passion fruit into a small pan and heating. It will take seconds to thicken up.

If you have any *Meringue shards* (page 219), serve them with this or leftover filo crisps from the *Passion fruit and raspberry millefeuille* (page 190).

Chestnut & chocolate parfait

You will have 150g chestnuts left over from a vacuum pack after making the *Cavolo nero and chestnut gnocchi with pecorino nero* (pages 156–157). Roughly chop the chestnuts, put in a mini processor with 2 tablespoons of icing sugar, a splash of rum, if you like, and 4 tablespoons of double cream from a 125ml carton. Whizz until smooth. Tip into a bowl and add a few chopped pecans, chop in a few

squares of dark chocolate and the remaining cream. Spoon into two 150ml dariole moulds, ramekins or espressso cups and keep in the fridge or freeze until 20 minutes before serving.

Apple with soft cheese

Core a Cox's apple and cut into 12 wedges, put a splash of olive oil in a frying pan and fry the apple until just golden. Scatter over 1 tablespoon of coconut palm sugar and add a knob of butter, turn the apple in the mixture until the wedges are sticky and soft. Add some slices of cold Vignotte, Chaource or clotted cream to serve.

Strawberries & honey

Take the ripest strawberries, cut in half straight into a dish, add some pomegranate seeds and cut a slab of honeycomb to go over the top. Add some coconut or natural yogurt and spoon over some saba or vincotta. Top with lavender, borage flowers or violas if you have them.

Wispy clouds in elderflower custard with syrup

Wispy clouds are my take on Iles Flottantes the soft poached meringues served on crème anglaise. You could make the custard and syrup in advance and gently heat before serving.

FOR THE CUSTARD

115ml *Elderflower cordial* (page 182)

1 large egg

2 tablespoons caster sugar

FOR THE SYRUP

100ml *Elderflower cordial* (page 182)

1½ tablespoons caster sugar

FOR THE WISPY CLOUDS

1 large egg white

pinch of sea salt crystals

45g caster sugar

WASTE NOT

If you have any leftover meringue mixture simply follow the recipe for Meringue shards (page 219) to bake them and store in an airtight container. They are fantastic to have to hand when you are after a quick dessert.

Before making the custard, put a few centimetres of cold water in a large bowl. (You will need this to halt the cooking process of the custard.)

Heat the cordial in a saucepan over a medium heat to just below boiling. Meanwhile, whisk the egg and sugar together and stir in the hot cordial. Pour the mixture back into the pan then return it to the lowest heat (this is important because you don't want scrambled eggs). Use a wooden spoon to stir the mixture continuously for about 2 minutes until thickened to the consistency of custard. Remove the pan from the heat and plunge the base of it into the bowl of cold water to halt the cooking process.

To make the syrup, put the cordial and sugar in a small saucepan and place over a low heat until the sugar has dissolved. Increase the heat and simmer for about 6 minutes until it thickens and turns pale golden in colour.

Now make the wispy clouds. Bring some water to the boil in a large pan with a lid. Put a double layer of kitchen paper onto a work surface. Whisk the egg whites with the salt to firm peaks then add the sugar, a little at a time, whisking well between each addition until you have meringue that is stiff, glossy and holds firm peaks. Then pour the custard into a dessert plate.

Reduce the heat and make sure the water is not moving. Use a teaspoon to scoop the meringue mixture and gently slide it onto the surface of the water, peaking it into a pointed shape. Make as many wispy clouds as you fancy eating (any leftover meringue mixture will not go to waste! See left). Cook them for 2 minutes, then lift out with a slotted spoon. Let each one drain on kitchen paper briefly before sliding each wispy cloud onto the custard. Spoon over the syrup and serve warm.

Almost

Instant

'Quality means doing it right when no one is looking.'

—

Henry Ford

Grilled goat's cheese, white peach & redcurrants

Summer savory, also known as the bean herb, is redolent of summer but you can grow winter savory, which is evergreen and slightly more pungent. Either one is perfect for this dish. If you have tender leaf thyme, this is a fine substitute. Buckler leaf sorrel is a lovely salad leaf with a lemony tang; once grown on your patch you'll always have it. The best goat's cheese to use for this recipe is with a rind, 4cm tall and 6cm in diameter.

4 teaspoons olive oil

20g butter

1 white-fleshed peach or nectarine, sliced into wedges

60g redcurrants, pulled from the stalks

2 sprigs summer savory (or thyme), with flowers if possible

2 tablespoons peach schnapps

1 x 100g goat's cheese with rind

small handful of buckler leaf sorrel, watercress or rocket, to serve

freshly ground black pepper

Heat 3 teaspoons of the oil and the butter in a frying pan over a medium–high heat and fry the peaches on both sides until softened and pale golden. Throw in the redcurrants and swirl the pan around to keep them moving. Pull the leaves from one savory sprig and add to the pan, pour in the schnapps and continue to cook for about a minute or until the juices turn syrupy.

Preheat the grill to high and arrange the rack 15cm from the heat. Line a small baking tray with foil. Halve the cheese horizontally and put on the foil, cut-side up. Pull the leaves off the remaining savory sprig straight over the cheese, grind over a little pepper and drizzle with the remaining teaspoon of oil.

Grill the goat's cheese for 3–4 minutes until golden and just bubbling at the edges. Serve right away along with the fruit and their juices spooned over. Scatter with savory flowers, if you have them, and buckler leaf sorrel or salad leaves.

Larb

This Laotian and northern Thai dish is the tastiest minced salad I know. I love how Thai cooks use raw rice that has been lightly toasted and ground (*khao khua*) as a seasoning to give texture and flavour. Adding deliciously aniseedy Thai basil lifts the dish to another flavour level.

In favour of speed, I've used ready-minced pork. But when I have more time, I will happily go for the purist approach and finely chop a piece of pork tenderloin. This dish also works very well with finely chopped chicken breast instead of pork. Serve with cellophane rice noodles, which are very fast to prepare following packet instructions.

250g fresh pork mince

finely grated zest and juice of 1 lime

2cm piece of fresh ginger, peeled and finely grated

1 tablespoon jasmine rice

6 small pink Thai shallots, red onions or shallots

5 spring onions

1 tablespoon sunflower oil

½ teaspoon coconut palm sugar

1 teaspoon red chilli flakes

1 tablespoon fish sauce

a few coriander leaves

a few sprigs of mint

a few sprigs of Thai basil

25g roasted salted peanuts, rinsed, dried and roughly chopped

Put the pork in a bowl, add the lime zest, half the juice and the ginger, stir well and set aside.

Toast the rice in a dry wok stirring all the time until golden, about 5 minutes. Transfer to a plate to cool and then finely grind using a pestle and mortar and set aside.

Thinly slice the pink shallots lengthways and the spring onions diagonally, keeping their green and white parts separate.

Heat a wok until it starts to smoke, add the oil followed by the pork mixture and stir-fry for 3 minutes until most of the liquid has evaporated. Add half the sliced pink shallots and the sugar and continue to fry for 2 minutes. Remove from the heat and add the chilli flakes, fish sauce, the white part of the spring onions and the ground rice. Stir well and add the green part of the spring onions. Chop half the herbs and add, along with the toasted peanuts. Serve right away with the remaining shallots and herb leaves and more chilli flakes if you wish.

Grilled halloumi, green beans, beetroot & mixed onion salad

Italian pink onions, around in July and August, can be found at greengrocers; they are milder than ordinary onions and pretty too. Or go for Bombay onions, available almost all year round in Indian and West Indian greengrocers as they also have a great flavour and a gentle pink colour.

a big handful of broad beans
  in pods

50g fine green beans

1 candy or golden beetroot, peeled

1 small pink onion, finely sliced

3 spring onions, finely sliced

125g halloumi, cut into 4 slices and
  patted dry with kitchen paper

FOR THE DRESSING

1 garlic clove, crushed to a paste
  with salt or 1 teaspoon *Crushed
  garlic* (page 207)

1 teaspoon white balsamic vinegar

a few sprigs of Greek basil, half the
  leaves chopped

2 tablespoons extra virgin olive oil

sea salt crystals and freshly ground
  black pepper

First make the dressing. Put the garlic, vinegar, the chopped basil, extra virgin olive oil, salt and pepper in a screw-top jar with a secure lid and shake vigorously to emulsify.

Pod the broad beans. Cook the green beans in a pan of salted boiling water for 3 minutes, then add the broad beans and cook for a further 2 minutes. Drain in a colander and refresh with cold running water. If the broad bean skins are very green they are fine, but if they have thick, pale skins, peel them. Slice the green beans in half lengthways then across into two. Pop the green beans and broad beans into a dish.

Slice the beetroot finely and add to the beans along with the onion and the spring onions. Pour over all but a spoonful of the dressing and toss together.

Heat a ridged griddle pan and griddle the halloumi for 1½ minutes on each side until golden. Place the halloumi on top of the salad and scatter with the remaining basil and dressing.

WASTE NOT

Use halloumi in *Seared halloumi with herb and saba dresssing on tahini yogurt* (page 18).

Watermelon, feta & rocket salad with beetroot vinaigrette

You could use a cantaloupe melon or other orange-fleshed varieties for this recipe, but I like the crazy colours you create when splashed with the beetroot dressing, Jackson Pollock style.

1 teaspoon Dijon mustard

1 tablespoon white balsamic vinegar

⅛ teaspoon beetroot powder

2 tablespoons olive oil

a thick wedge of mini watermelon, skin removed and cut into thin slices

50g feta, shaved

60g coppa stagionata (a traditional salami from Umbria) or prosciutto de Parma

a handful of wild or broad-leaved rocket

First make the vinaigrette. Put the mustard, vinegar, beetroot powder and oil in a screw-top jar with a secure lid and shake vigorously to emulsify.

Put the watermelon on a plate with the shaved feta, coppa stagionata and rocket. Wildly splatter over the dressing and serve.

WASTE NOT

Use the remaining watermelon in place of the papaya to make a Watermelon and yogurt sherbet (see page 188). The feta can be used for *Farro with spinach, feta and olives* (page 84).

Borscht my style

This is a satisfying soup not just taste wise but colour wise too. It cocoons goodness – just what you need on a chilly night. Go crazy with the toppings; you can try the suggestion in the recipe or try grilled goat's cheese on top of a toasted slice of baguette or a blob of horseradish cream and a zigzag of saba. Take enough soup to eat right away, leave some for the next day, freeze the rest for next week or have friends round for supper and eat the lot.

MAKES 3–4 SERVINGS

2 tablespoons olive oil

20g salted butter

1 medium pink or red onion

3 garlic cloves, finely chopped

6 small–medium beetroots (or about 500g beetroots), scrubbed or peeled

1 small red-skinned potato, thinly sliced

a small strip of orange rind

1 teaspoon beetroot powder (optional)

500ml vegetable stock

375ml boiling water from the kettle

150ml crème fraîche

3 tablespoons hot horseradish sauce

sea salt crystals and freshly ground pepper

FOR THE TOPPING

a few beetroot leaves (optional)

100g feta, cut into chunks

splash of extra virgin olive oil

beetroot powder, to dust (optional)

Heat the oil and butter in a large lidded pan over a low–medium heat, add the onion and garlic then sweat for 5 minutes.

Cut the beetroots in half and slice them thinly then add them to the onions and garlic. Do the same with the potato, then add it with the orange rind and stir to coat everything in the oil. Pop the lid on and sweat for a further 5 minutes over a low heat. Add the beetroot powder (if using) and pour in the stock and the boiling water, season with salt and pepper and increase the heat to bring it up to a simmer. Half-cover with a lid and cook gently for 25 minutes, or until the beetroot is just tender.

Meanwhile, if using beetroot leaves, preheat the oven to 180°C/gas mark 4. Wash and dry well and lay the leaves out on a rack set on a baking tray. Place in the oven to dry them out for 5 minutes. Reduce the heat to 100°C/gas mark ¼ and dry for a further 3–5 minutes until crispy. Lift the rack onto a board and set aside to cool.

Add the crème fraîche and horseradish sauce to the soup and leave to cool a little. Blend in a mini food processor or blender, in batches, to a smooth purée, tasting to adjust the seasoning.

Preheat the grill to high. Put chunks of feta on a foil-lined tray and grill for a few minutes until golden – if you own a blowtorch you could use this to sear the feta instead. To serve, spoon the soup into a bowl, top with grilled feta, a few splashes of extra virgin olive oil, dust with beetroot powder (if using) and crumple over some of the crisp beetroot leaves.

Farro with spinach, feta & olives

This dish is based on the Greek national favourite *Spanakorizo* – rice and spinach. It can be made with orzo pasta too but I make it with farro, the Italian hard wheat or whole spelt grain, which is a useful staple to have cooked ready in the fridge for other occasions. You could add cooked prawns or a bit of canned tuna along with any leftover roasted vegetables (page 89) but I love it as it is with feta and olives and perhaps a fresh sardine simply grilled when in season.

100g farro

6 Kalamata olives

1 small onion, finely chopped

3 tablespoons olive oil

160g spinach

½ teaspoon sea salt crystals

20g fresh dill, thick stems removed and sprigs roughly chopped

finely grated zest of 1 lemon, plus juice of ½ lemon

50g feta, crumbled roughly

extra virgin olive oil, to serve

Soak the farro in a bowl of cold water for 20 minutes.

Meanwhile, cut the flesh from the olive stones lengthways and set aside.

Drain the farro and put in a small pan with 200ml cold water. Bring to the boil, part cover with a lid and simmer gently for 5–7 minutes until almost cooked.

Meanwhile, put the onion and oil in a medium pan and cook over a low heat for 3 minutes without browning. Increase the heat a little and add half the spinach and stir to wilt. When there is just enough room in the pan for the remaining spinach, add with a pinch of salt, the chopped dill, farro and its liquid and the lemon juice.

Bring back to a gentle simmer then reduce the heat to very low and cook for a further 5 minutes until the liquid has almost all been absorbed. Remove from the heat, stir in the lemon zest, cover and leave for 10 minutes. Put half aside in a container to cool completely and then refrigerate to eat another time. Serve the rest straightaway with the feta and olives folded through and a little extra virgin olive oil trickled over the top.

WASTE NOT

Any leftover feta can be used in *Chickpeas in tomato sauce with feta and parsley* (page 135) and *Watermelon, feta and rocket salad with beetroot vinaigrette* (page 80).

Baked hake, potatoes, olives & lemon

Thank goodness hake is now being sold outside of Spain. It's a wonderfully delicious fish if cooked well. This oven-baked favourite makes a quick autumn weekend meal. If you don't have any bread handy for making breadcrumbs, buy ready-made fresh breadcrumbs from the chiller in the supermarket, not the dry packet sort, and freeze what you don't use.

1 x 200g hake fillet or chunky haddock or cod with skin, cut in half

325g or 2 medium red-skinned potatoes

4 tablespoons olive oil

2–3 tablespoons fresh breadcrumbs

1 teaspoon hot paprika

1 small garlic clove crushed to a paste with a little salt or ½ teaspoon *Crushed garlic* (page 207)

5 fronds of flat-leaf parsley, finely chopped

¼ small lemon, cut into 4 wedges

8 pitted Greek Kalamata olives

sea salt crystals and freshly ground black pepper

cooked green beans or chard, cooked as for the *Cod fillet with rainbow chard and sobrasada* (page 59), to serve

Season the fish with a little salt on both sides and transfer to the fridge. This is best done as soon as you buy it, even if you are using it right away as it firms up the flesh but especially if you are cooking with it the next day.

Preheat the oven to 200°C/gas mark 6.

Thinly slice the potatoes using a mandolin or very sharp knife and season with salt and pepper. Grease a deep, approx. 23 x 18cm ovenproof dish with a little oil and layer up the sliced potatoes. Spoon over a little of the oil and a little cold water as you go. Bake for 30–40 minutes until just tender.

Meanwhile, mix the breadcrumbs, paprika, garlic and parsley together and set aside.

Rinse the salt off the fish under the cold tap (if you have done this the day before) and pat dry with kitchen paper. Slash the skin side on both pieces a couple of times and sprinkle with pepper.

Insert a wedge of lemon into each slash and lay the fish over the part-cooked potatoes. Pour 2 tablespoons of water around the sides of the dish to moisten. Then sprinkle over the breadcrumb mixture, avoiding the skin of the fish, and spoon over the remaining olive oil. Slide the dish into the oven and cook for 10 minutes.

Remove from the oven and scatter the olives over and around the fish then cook for a further 5 minutes until the fish is just flaky and the potatoes are cooked through. Serve right away with cooked green beans or chard.

Prawn & squash salad with *nam jim* dressing

This is a salad with the wonderfully addictive *nam jim* – a Thai dipping sauce that is often served with seafood – and this is just one of many variations. As in all Thai cooking the key elements are there: hot, sour, salty and sweet. You won't use all of it so put the leftover sauce in a jar and store it in the fridge ready to serve another time with any non-oily fish or chicken or try it dressed over kale – it perks up many a dish.

50–75g sugar snap peas or mangetout, sliced in half lengthways

⅓ portion of *Roasted butternut squash and pumpkin* (page 124)

1 tablespoon sunflower oil

100g raw prawns, shelled and tails left intact

2 spring onions, sliced diagonally

FOR THE *NAM JIM*

2 tablespoons coconut palm sugar

2 garlic cloves, finely chopped

2cm piece of fresh ginger, peeled and finely grated

2 small Thai shallots or 1 small banana shallot, finely chopped

3 tablespoons fish sauce

about 10g coriander sprigs, roughly chopped

juice of 2 large limes (about 50ml juice)

2 fat red chillies, deseeded (if you don't like it hot) and finely chopped

TO SERVE

20g toasted cashews

a handful of coriander leaves

wedge of lime

To make the *nam jim*, put all the ingredients, leaving aside one of the chopped chillies, in a mini food processor (or use a pestle and mortar) and whizz to combine to a chunky sauce.

In a pan of salted boiling water, blanch the sugar snaps for 1 minute, then drain, refresh under cold running water, drain again, put in a bowl and set aside. Slice or scoop off the skin from the roasted squash if roasted with skin on. Add to the sugar snaps.

Heat a wok over a high heat and when the pan is smoking, add the oil followed by the prawns. Stir-fry for 2 minutes and, once the prawns are seared, add the spring onions and stir-fry until the prawns are just pink and cooked through. Add the roasted squash and sugar snaps, stir to heat through. Spoon over about half the *nam jim* and toss together. Top with the remaining chopped chilli, the cashews and coriander leaves and serve with a lime wedge.

Tray-roasted vegetables & crispy parsley leaves with salsa salmoriglio

I love these jewel-like vegetables served with my favourite sauce from Sicily, salmoriglio. I like to make it with pink Himalayan salt (although any good flaky salt will do). *Salamoia*, meaning salty in Italian, is how this sauce came to be named. You could use a few salted anchovies finely chopped in the sauce instead of the salt along with some chilli flakes – very Roman and very good!

250g piece celeriac (half a small root), cut into 10 wedges

1 fennel bulb, cut into 6 lengthways

1 red pepper, deseeded and cut into 10 pieces

2–3 small red or pink onions, halved

1 pale green baton courgette, cut into 4 lengthways

1 garlic clove, sliced

2 tablespoons olive oil

pink Himalayan salt crystals and freshly ground black pepper

about 10 flat-leaf parsley leaves

12 cherry tomatoes on the vine

FOR THE SALSA SALMORIGLIO

4 tablespoons extra virgin olive oil

juice of ½ lemon

2 garlic cloves, finely chopped

about 10g flat-leaf parsley

3 sprigs marjoram or oregano

½ teaspoon pink Himalayan salt crystals, roughly crushed

¼ teaspoon freshly ground black pepper

To make the salsa salmoriglio, put the oil and lemon juice in a bowl, whisk in 2 tablespoons of water and add the garlic. Chop the parsley and marjoram (or oregano) together and add to the bowl with the salt and pepper.

Preheat the oven to 220°C/gas mark 7.

In a pan of boiling water, blanch the celeriac for a minute and leave to drain in a colander. Put the remaining prepared vegetables (except the parsley and tomatoes) in a large shallow roasting tin, add the oil and seasoning with the celeriac and toss together then lay the veggies out so that they don't overlap.

Roast for 25–30 minutes, adding the parsley and tomatoes for the last 5 minutes. (It helps if you open the oven door to let the steam escape from time to time during roasting so the vegetables don't steam.) Serve with the salsa salmoriglio.

Pumpkin & cavolo nero with goat's cheese & polpetti

Instead of fresh pork you could use good-quality skinned sausage meat for the polpetti (just omit the egg yolk). Stripping the soft leaves from the cavolo nero is easy – just grab either side of the stem end and pull.

½–1 portion of *Roasted butternut squash and pumpkin* (page 124)

150g cavolo nero, leaves stripped from the thick stems and torn

1 garlic clove crushed to a paste with a little salt or 1 teaspoon *Crushed garlic* (page 207)

large pinch of Espelette pepper

60g soft goat's cheese

finely grated zest of 1 small orange

2 tablespoons toasted cashews

extra virgin olive oil, to serve

sea salt crystals

FOR THE POLPETTI

250g pork mince

1 small egg yolk

1 tablespoon *Tapenade* (page 198)

a small bunch of flat-leaf parsley, leaves removed and chopped

1 tablespoon olive oil

pinch of sea salt crystals and freshly ground black pepper

Preheat the oven to 190°C/gas mark 5.

Put all the ingredients for the polpetti, except the oil, in a bowl. Mix with your hands to form a smooth paste and form into about 10 balls. Heat the oil in a frying pan over a medium heat and cook the balls for 4 minutes until golden, turning as they cook. Reduce the heat and fry for a further 2 minutes until just cooked through.

Meanwhile, cook the cavolo nero. Heat the remaining oil in a large wok and add the garlic, as it fizzes add the cavolo nero, stir-fry it for a minute. Add a splash of water, cover with a lid and wilt the leaves for 2 minutes. Add a pinch of salt and Espelette pepper. Put the pumpkin, cavolo nero and as many polpetti as you like in a dish and top with goat's cheese, some orange zest and the toasted cashews. Finish with some extra virgin olive oil.

WASTE NOT

Use any excess polpetti in the *Rich tomato sauce* (page 127) and wilt in some spinach. Butternut squash can be used in *Prawn and squash salad with nam jim dressing* (page 86) and cavolo nero for *Cavolo nero and chestnut gnocchi with percorino nero* (pages 156–157).

Roasted cauliflower, fennel & chorizo puchero with quinoa

To heat the cooked quinoa, I like to use my collapsible wire basket. Once hot, mix with everything in the roasting tin and serve from that. Crispy kale is also tasty served as a nibble with padrón peppers and chorizo puchero (tiny cocktail-style chorizo).

50g curly kale, leaves stripped and stems discarded

3 tablespoons olive oil

4 or more chorizo puchero

½ small cauliflower, broken into small florets

1 small fennel, sliced lengthways

6 small padrón peppers or tiny coloured peppers

sea salt crystals

½ portion cooked *Quinoa* (page 130)

Preheat the oven to 200°C/gas mark 6. Put the kale in a shallow roasting tin and coat with ½ teaspoon of the oil and bake for 5 minutes. Tip onto a plate and set aside.

Put the chorizo puchero in a small bowl, pour over boiling water and leave for 5 minutes then drain, dry and set aside.

Increase the oven temperature to 220°C/gas mark 7. Put the cauliflower and fennel in a roasting tin and toss with 1 tablespoon of the oil. Put in the oven to roast for 10 minutes turning them halfway through.

Add the chorizo puchero and padrón peppers to the tin, coat with the remaining oil and return to the oven for 10 minutes until everything is tinged golden. Scatter a little sea salt over the vegetables. Steam the quinoa in a bowl to heat through and serve along with the crispy kale and roasted vegetables.

WASTE NOT

For more with kale, cauliflower and quinoa, see *Curly kale ash* (page 206), *Seared scallops and cauliflower crumbs with garlic, chilli and herb butter* (page 48) and *Lunchtime verrine* (page 118).

Roast chicken breast, tomatoes, butterbeans & Savoy cabbage

You could use fresh or canned borlotti beans instead of butterbeans for this recipe if you have them. Kale or chard are also good substitutes for the Savoy cabbage or simply fold spinach through the beans and tomato to wilt into the pan juices.

1–2 chicken breasts, skin on

1–2 tomatoes, each cut into 6 pieces

2 tablespoons olive oil

200g canned butterbeans or borlotti beans

1 small Savoy cabbage

1 portion of *Tarragon and hazelnut pesto* (page 201)

extra virgin olive oil, to serve

sea salt crystals and freshly ground black pepper

Preheat the oven to 200°C/gas mark 6.

Season the chicken with salt and pepper and place in a small roasting tin. Tuck the tomato pieces under and around the chicken and spoon over 1 tablespoon of the olive oil. Roast for 30 minutes until cooked through and golden. Remove from the oven and leave to rest for 5 minutes.

Meanwhile, rinse and drain the butterbeans and put in a small pan with the remaining olive oil. Add the tomatoes and juices from the roasting tin and set over a low heat to warm through for a couple of minutes.

Slice the cabbage into four wedges, leaving the root end intact, salt lightly and steam as much as you want over a pan of boiling water for 4 minutes. Lift the cabbage onto a side plate, spoon over the extra virgin olive oil and serve alongside the beans and tomatoes, the chicken breast and the tarragon and hazelnut pesto.

WASTE NOT

To use up the butterbeans and the remaining cabbage from this recipe, make a soup. Simply sweat 1 finely chopped onion in a pan with a little olive oil and add 1 teaspoon of *Crushed garlic* (page 207). Throw in 2 chopped tomatoes and cook for 5 minutes. Add the butterbeans, 350ml chicken stock (page 179) and simmer for 10 minutes. Shred the cabbage and add to the pan and continue to simmer for a further 5 minutes. Serve hot with grissini, if you like.

Smashed potatoes, chicken balls, crispy gremolata & radicchio

If you have a couple of raw sausages in your fridge, by all means use those instead of the chicken. Just remove their skins and use them as mincemeat. I find it useful to cook enough potatoes for two meals so cook double the quantity. Fry them up or steam them to serve with a multitude of dishes over a busy week.

200g medium King Edward potatoes (or whatever you have in your cupboard)

3½ tablespoons olive oil

1 small radicchio, trevise, chicory or Little Gem, cut in half

FOR THE CHICKEN BALLS

1 large chicken breast, skinned

5g parsley leaves, stripped off stalks and finely chopped

½ teaspoon smoked garlic powder

1 tablespoon plain flour

2 teaspoons finely grated Parmesan

sea salt crystals and freshly ground white pepper

FOR THE GREMOLATA

10g parsley leaves, stripped off stalks and finely chopped

finely grated zest of 1 unwaxed lemon

1 garlic clove, crushed with a little salt or 1 teaspoon *Crushed garlic* (page 207)

1 tablespoon olive oil

pinch of sea salt crystals

1 slice of bread, crusts removed and finely chopped or put in a mini processor and whizzed to a rough crumb

Cut the potatoes into quarters and cook in a pan of salted boiling water for 10 minutes or until just tender. Remove from the heat and drain in a colander.

Preheat the oven to 180°C/gas mark 4.

Make the chicken balls. Cut the chicken into cubes and blitz in a mini food processor with the parsley and salt and white pepper until you have a rough paste. Use dampened hands to form the mixture into six balls. Mix the smoked garlic powder with the flour on a plate and roughly coat the balls in this mixture.

Next, make the gremolata by mixing all the ingredients together in a bowl. Heat a frying pan over a medium heat and add the mixture, stir for 2–3 minutes until golden and crispy. Tip into a bowl.

Roughly crush the potatoes with a fork to break them up a little. Heat 2 tablespoons of the oil in the frying pan and fry the potatoes until golden and crispy. Tip onto a plate and wipe out the pan with kitchen paper.

Heat 1 tablespoon of oil in the same pan over a medium–high heat and sear the chicken balls to get a good even colour on all sides. Pop the pan into the oven (cover the handle with foil if it's likely to burn or melt). Cook the balls for about 5 minutes. Throw the golden-fried potatoes into the pan then turn off the oven and leave to keep warm.

Heat a ridged griddle pan or a frying pan until smoking hot and spoon the remaining oil over the cut-side of the radicchio halves and sear them for a few minutes. Turn and cook for a further minute. Arrange on a plate, add the potatoes and chicken balls and scatter with the crispy gremolata.

Prawn, cod & courgette fritters

Ideally, use fish that you have already salted in the fridge but if you haven't done this, salting it about 30 minutes or so before cooking will be fine. Salting the courgette gets rid of the moisture but they need a mighty squeeze to get rid of all the excess moisture before you add them to the fritter mix.

FOR THE FRITTERS

120g cod or pollock fillet (preferably salted in the fridge overnight)

about 80g raw prawns, shelled

2 teaspoons coconut flour or potato flour

2 spring onions, chopped

1 medium egg

1 medium courgette (weighing no more than 200g)

1 tablespoon sunflower oil

½ packet ready-cooked beluga lentils or ½ portion *Puy lentils* (page 121)

1 tablespoons olive oil

2 spring onions, finely sliced

sea salt crystals and freshly ground black pepper

TO SERVE

a big handful of wild rocket, including some flowers if available

2 tablespoons *Mustard and white balsamic vinaigrette* (page 207)

Put the fish into a non-corrosive dish, sprinkle with sea salt crystals and leave in the fridge for at least 30 minutes. If you're using already salted fish, follow the recipe below.

Rinse the fish and roughly chop, along with the prawns. Put in a mini food processor with the flour, spring onions, egg and a small pinch of salt and pepper. Whizz to make a paste, tip into a bowl and chill for about 1 hour.

Meanwhile, grate the courgette on the large holes of a box grater and put in a colander set over a bowl. Fold through a few pinches of salt and set aside to drain for about 40 minutes.

Squeeze the courgette in batches until no more liquid comes out and mix into the chilled fish mixture. Divide into six fritter-shaped rounds, roughly the same size.

Heat the sunflower oil in a large non-stick frying pan over a medium heat and fry the fritters for 3–4 minutes on each side, using a spoon to baste the fritters with the oil as they fry. Check that they are cooked right through – if they require further cooking, reduce the heat to low and continue to cook for another couple of minutes. Lift the fritters onto a plate lined with kitchen paper. Eat what you want right away, allow the rest to cool completely, then store in a container in the fridge for up to 24 hours.

Meanwhile, rinse the lentils in cold water if using shop-bought, ready-cooked beluga. Heat the olive oil in a pan and fry the spring onions for a few seconds, then add the lentils to heat through. Arrange the lentils and fritters on a serving plate, add the rocket and spoon over the vinaigrette to serve.

WASTE NOT

For more with cod or pollock see *Goan fish curry*, page 107. Use the remaining beluga or *Puy lentils* for *Lunchtime verrine* (page 118).

Smoked halibut sashimi with yuzu sesame dressing & wasabi jelly

Instead of halibut I often use smoked eel for this dish and smoked salmon works well too, maybe with the remaining salmon roe left over from the *Runner beans with smoked salmon* (page 137). You could also use raw sashimi if you have access to spanking fresh fish. I like to use agar flakes for the wasabi jelly as it sets so fast; you only need a small amount of jelly to add a little excitement to this treat of a dish so use the remainder in half an avocado dressed with soy suace and sesame oil. Mikawa mirin is a fermented and aged sweet rice wine.

1 tablespoon hijiki seaweed

2 teaspoons mikawa mirin

2 teaspoons light soy sauce

pinch of coconut palm sugar

40g frozen podded edamame (or use fresh, if available)

200g packet thinly sliced smoked halibut (smoked eel or salmon are also good)

85g black or brown rice noodles

red and green shiso leaves (optional)

a few pieces of pickled ginger

micro coriander leaves (optional)

pinch of sea salt crystals

FOR THE WASABI JELLY

1½ teaspoons agar flakes

2 teaspoons wasabi paste

FOR THE DRESSING

1 tablespoon soy sauce

2 teaspoons yuzu juice (or lime juice)

1 teaspoon sesame oil

First make the jelly. Pour 75ml cold water into a small pan and sprinkle over the agar flakes, heat gently without being tempted to stir. Once it is just simmering, stir gently for a minute until the liquid looks clear. Put the wasabi in a small bowl and add a little of the liquid, stir until smooth then add the remaining liquid. Pour into a small container or mini loaf tin that will comfortably fit in a bowl. Pour cold water into the bowl and sit the container in it for about 5 minutes to allow the jelly to cool and set.

Put the hijiki seaweed in a bowl and cover with boiling water and leave for 5 minutes. Drain and add the mirin, light soy sauce, sugar and 1 tablespoon of cold water.

To make the dressing, whisk the soy sauce, yuzu juice and the sesame oil together in a small bowl and set aside.

Cook the edamame in a pan of boiling water for 5 minutes, drain and refresh under cold running water and drain again.

Arrange the halibut on a plate with the edamame. Cut the jelly into cubes – you might not need it all – and add to the fish or serve in a small bowl.

Now cook the noodles. Put them upright in a small pan over a medium–high heat, add a pinch of salt and pour over boiling water from the kettle to half fill the pan. As the water boils, separate the strands with a fork and cook for about 3½ minutes or to your liking, drain and refresh with hot water then cold and put in a small bowl with the shiso if using. Pour the juices from the hijiki over the noodles to moisten them a little.

To serve, sprinkle the fish with the seaweed, spoon over the dressing and add the pickled ginger. Scatter with the micro coriander leaves if using and serve with the noodles.

Seared tuna with quinoa, mangetout & cucumber salad

Quinoa is a fantastic grain that is available in lots of different colours – wholefood and healthfood shops stock a variety so you can either make up your own assortment or buy the tricolore in a pack.

Violas are a thing of beauty to grow in pots for many months of the year. They are really worth trying as they add a touch of prettiness to the simplest plate of food.

60g tricolore quinoa

1 x 2.5cm thick piece of fresh tuna

3 tablespoons olive oil

juice of 1 orange

50g mangetout

8–10 French breakfast or mixed coloured radishes, sliced

10cm piece of cucumber, peeled in strips, deseeded and halved lengthways

sea salt flakes and freshly ground black pepper

violas or other edible flowers (optional), to serve

Rinse the quinoa and put in a pan with 150ml cold water. Bring to the boil then reduce the heat and cook for 8 minutes. Remove from the heat and leave, covered, for 20 minutes. Season with salt and pepper and tip into a dish to cool completely.

Coat the tuna in 1 teaspoon of olive oil and season with salt and pepper.

Put the remaining oil in a bowl and whisk in the orange juice and season.

Cook the mangetout in salted boiling water for 2 minutes, drain in a colander and refresh in cold water. Pile a few together at a time and slice into 3 lengthways. Put them in a serving dish with the quinoa, radishes and cucumber and pour over the orange dressing.

Heat a ridged grill pan over a high heat until just smoking, reduce the heat and sear the tuna for 2 minutes on the first side and 1 minute on the other for rare or cook to your liking. Remove and let the tuna rest on a plate for 5 minutes before slicing and laying on top of the salad. To serve, scatter with a few violas or other edible flowers.

Paprika & salt-crusted monkfish & padrón pepper skewers

The skewers are served with pebre, the Chilean sauce that varies between each household. Monkfish is considered a rather pricey fish but is an ideal treat for the solo diner. Its meaty texture makes it great for skewering and soaking up the subtle-barbecue flavour of the salt. Salish salt, used in this recipe, is slowly smoked over red alder branches in the North Pacific Indian tradition, turning the salt into a wonderful pearly, pinky grey shade – the colour of a good caviar.

1½ teaspoons smoked hot paprika

½ teaspoon Salish smoked salt or sea salt crystals, lightly crushed

300–400g monkfish tail fillets, skinned

6 padrón peppers or small coloured peppers

1 tablespoon olive oil

FOR THE CUCUMBER AND MINT SAUCE

75ml natural yogurt

½ Lebanese cucumber

5 large sprigs of mint

FOR THE PEBRE

¼ pink or red onion (pink Bombay onions are good), finely chopped

1 *Grilled marinated red pepper*, finely chopped (page 200)

1 fat red chilli, deseeded and finely chopped

1 teaspoon *Raspberry Vinegar* (page 213) or shop-bought raspberry vinegar

1 tablespoon extra virgin olive oil

2 tomatoes, halved, cored, roughly deseeded and chopped

a small bunch of coriander, leaves finely chopped

sea salt crystals and freshly ground black pepper

Mix the paprika and Salish salt together in a small bowl and rub this generously into the fish then set aside for 15 minutes. Cut the fillets into about 3.5cm pieces and thread onto two metal skewers, alternating with a few padrón peppers.

Preheat the grill to high and set the rack about 15cm from the heat.

Line a baking tray with foil and put a small wire rack on top. Lay the skewers on the rack, spoon over the

oil and grill for 5 minutes. Move the rack up a little and grill closer to the heat for a further 3 minutes. Rest the skewers for 5 minutes.

Meanwhile, make the cucumber and mint sauce. Put the yogurt in a mini food processor. Peel some of the cucumber but leave some green bits to give the sauce some colour then slice it in half, deseed it and pop straight into the yogurt. Whizz to a purée and tip into a small bowl. Tear the leaves off the mint sprigs and finely chop, then add to the purée, season with salt and pepper and set aside.

To make the pebre, mix all the ingredients together in a bowl. Serve the skewers with the pebre and cucumber and mint sauce alongside.

WASTE NOT

Use any remaining padron peppers in *Roasted cauliflower, fennel and chorizo puchero with quinoa* (page 93).

Goan fish curry

This curry makes enough for a solo dinner plus another meal, which could be 24 hours later if kept chilled. Serve the curry with freshly cooked jasmine rice or *Coconut pancakes* (page 134) to make it go further. I will often have salted fish on hand in the fridge, which makes life easier, otherwise you'll just need to salt it for 20–30 minutes before cooking. Curry leaves are wonderful and best used fresh – so if you have too many to use up share amongst your neighbours!

This dish requires you have some ready-cooked tomatoes with chickpeas from the Mezze (page 135).

150g skinless pollock or cod fillet

1 lime, ½ juiced the other ½ cut into wedges

1 tablespoon sunflower oil

1 pink, Bombay or white onion, finely chopped

3 garlic cloves, finely grated

3cm piece of fresh ginger, peeled and grated

1 long green chilli, deseeded and finely chopped

4 fresh curry leaves

¼ teaspoon turmeric

150ml canned coconut cream

50g dwarf beans, topped and tailed, halved lengthways then sliced in half across

Chickpeas in tomato sauce (page 135)

100g young spinach leaves

sea salt crystals

If you're using already salted fish, soak or rinse well depending on how long it has been salted, otherwise salt fresh fish 20–30 minutes before cooking to firm up the flesh. After this time, rinse and pour over the lime juice. Set aside while you prepare the remaining ingredients.

Heat the oil in a heavy-bottomed pan over a medium–low heat. Add the onion, garlic, ginger, chilli and curry leaves. Sweat for 4 minutes. Add the turmeric and the coconut cream from the can. Fill the empty can with cold water, swirl and pour into the pan. Increase the heat a little and bring to a gentle simmer for 5 minutes.

Meanwhile, lift the fish from the lime juice and cut into 3cm pieces then add to the pan along with the juice. Add the beans and cook over a low heat for 7 minutes.

Put the chickpeas in tomato sauce in a small pan and add the spinach. Stir to heat through and to wilt the spinach then add to the curry and serve.

Runner bean, new potato, courgette & lightly smoked salmon salad

Here is a garden or allotment salad full of summer flavours. Add marigold petals (*Calendula*) to the mix as they add their own flavour. If you have any runner beans that have toughened up and have fat beans inside their pods, remove the beans and cook, then skin them to reveal their bright green interior and use them in the salad too. You could use trofie, my favourite pasta, instead of the potatoes.

6 young runner beans (about 50g), plus any large older beans, podded

125g new potatoes

1 lightly smoked salmon fillet

10g salted butter

1 pale green baton courgette (available from Middle Eastern stores) or 1 medium yellow courgette

1 marigold flower head

FOR THE SWEET MUSTARD DRESSING

2 teaspoons Dijon mustard

¼ teaspoon caster sugar

1½ tablespoons white balsamic vinegar

3 tablespoons cold-pressed organic rapeseed oil

First make the sweet mustard dressing. Put all the ingredients into a screw-top jar with a secure lid and shake vigorously to emulsify.

Preheat the oven to 200°C/gas mark 6. String the beans using a vegetable peeler and slice them diagonally into thin shreds.

Cook the potatoes in salted boiling water for about 15 minutes until just cooked. Drain, peel if wished, and slice into rounds straight into a dish. Add half the dressing while still warm so they absorb the flavour.

Line a baking tray with foil and add the fish. Top with a knob of butter and cook in the oven for 9 minutes. Remove and allow the fish to cool briefly. Peel off the skin and flake into large pieces over the potatoes.

Cook the shredded beans and any whole podded beans in salted boiling water for 3–4 minutes until just tender, drain in a colander and refresh with cold running water. Pop any whole beans from their skins.

Meanwhile, slice the courgette thinly on the diagonal and toss into the dish with the beans and the remaining dressing. Pull the petals off the marigold flower straight over the dish and serve.

WASTE NOT

If you buy 2 lightly smoked salmon fillets (they often come in packs of two), use for *Pickled cucumber* (see page 128).

Smoked trout with black rice noodles, broccoli & Asian pesto

This is a useful way to use up any leftover Thai basil bought for the *Larb* (page 77). The pesto will keep for four days in a jar if covered with a slick of oil (which will preserve the bright green colour) and stored in the fridge. A bar of hard coconut is a useful ingredient as it keeps in the fridge for months. But pure coconut yogurt works well.

½ head broccoli

1 tablespoon sunflower oil

½ red chilli, deseeded and finely chopped

2 spring onions, finely sliced diagonally

80–100g black rice noodles or gluten-free noodles of choice

1 x fillet hot-smoked trout

FOR THE ASIAN PESTO

about 30g Thai basil leaves

3 tablespoons roasted peanuts (if salted rinse them)

pinch of pul biber pepper flakes

2 garlic cloves, crushed to a paste with a little salt or 2 teaspoons *Crushed garlic* (page 207)

100ml sunflower oil

3 tablespoons creamed coconut, grated from a hard bar or coconut yogurt

1 teaspoon fish sauce or more to taste

Put all the ingredients for the pesto in a mini food processor, blitz to a rough paste and put in a bowl.

Break the broccoli into small florets, peel and slice the fat stem. Heat the oil in a wok and fry the chilli. After 30 seconds add the broccoli florets, stems and spring onions and stir-fry for 1 minute.

Meanwhile, cook the noodles following the packet instructions then drain, add to the broccoli and toss with a few tablespoons of the Asian pesto. Flake over the trout fillet and eat straightaway.

WASTE NOT

Use up coconut yogurt in *Apricot and blueberry verrine with honeysuckle blossom* (page 66) or *Nectarine, passion fruit syrup and coconut yogurt* (page 69) and any leftover broccoli florets and stem can be added to *Lunchtime verrine* (page 118).

Crab, courgette & maftoul salad with brown crab mayonnaise

If you grow your own vegetables, this is a something-for-nothing meal as you can use whatever beans you have and courgettes even if they have overgrown a little. Maftoul is the giant Palestinian couscous, which needs slightly different treatment to ordinary couscous. It's sold in Middle Eastern shops or large supermarkets but if you can't easily find maftoul, use fregola sarda or if you have any leftover rice, this could be used instead, thrown in at the end.

1 tablespoon olive oil

50g maftoul or fregola sarda

3 tablespoons extra virgin olive oil

juice and finely grated zest of 1 lemon

5 small runner beans

1 small yellow and 1 small green courgette

1 small dressed crab (or 100g pack white and brown crabmeat)

2 tablespoons good-quality mayonnaise

micro red amaranth leaves, salad or herb leaves

sea salt crystals and freshly ground black pepper

Heat the olive oil in a frying pan over a medium heat and stir-fry the maftoul for 3 minutes. Add 125ml cold water and season with salt. Bring to a simmer for a few minutes until all the water is absorbed. Add a further 100ml water, bring to a simmer again and cook for a further 4 minutes, then remove from the heat. Add 1 tablespoon of extra virgin olive oil and half the lemon juice, cover and set aside for 10 minutes.

Meanwhile, string the beans using a vegetable peeler and slice diagonally into thin shreds. Cook in a saucepan of salted boiling water for 3 minutes until just tender. Drain in a colander and refresh with cold water. Slice the courgettes thinly and put in a bowl along with the runner beans.

Mix the lemon zest, remaining lemon juice and extra virgin olive oil and black pepper in a small bowl, and add this to the maftoul along with the white crabmeat. Mix the brown crabmeat into the mayonnaise. Serve the salad with the brown crab mayonnaise and scatter over some micro amaranth leaves, if you have them, or other small leaves.

WASTE NOT

You can also use maftoul in *Vine-leaf roasted quail stuffed with maftoul* (page 150).

Pistachio tarts

I like to use nibbed pistachios, which are shelled, skinned and sliced lengthways. They are a dramatic bright green colour. Find them in Middle Eastern shops but you can of course use shelled, skinned, whole pistachios if need be.

MAKES 6

65g nibbed pistachios, finely ground

6 sheets filo pastry (about 120g)

50g salted butter, melted, plus extra for greasing

65g caster sugar

4 tablespoons double cream

2 medium eggs

finely grated zest of 1 small orange

1 tablespoon self-raising flour

icing sugar, to dust

Preheat the oven to 200°C/gas mark 6 and grease a six-hole muffin tin with melted butter.

Grind the pistachios finely in a mini food processor.

Lay out one sheet of the filo and brush with some melted butter making sure to leave the whey behind. Put another sheet on top and repeat to make three layers. Cut out squares large enough to fit the holes in the muffin tin. Gently ease the filo squares into the holes and trim the excess with scissors to make a rough circle.

Put the sugar and 3 tablespoons of just-boiled water into a small saucepan over a low heat. Let the sugar dissolve to form a clear syrup then increase the heat and simmer until it turns a pale caramel colour. Remove from the heat, add the cream and stir well. Set aside to cool for 5 minutes.

Whisk the eggs until pale and creamy, gradually and carefully pour in the caramel while whisking, and add the orange zest. Sift over the flour and whisk in. Mix in the ground pistachios, spoon equally into the pastry and bake for 20 minutes until risen and firm. If it looks as though it is over-browning, cover the tin with foil and continue to bake until the filo is crisp and golden. Remove and cool in the tin for a minute then carefully lift out with the aid of a spatula and cool on a wire rack. Just before serving, dust liberally with icing sugar.

WASTE NOT

Any remaining filo sheets can be used to make *Passion fruit and raspberry millefeuille* (page 190).

A Little

Ahead

'Cooking is like love. It should be entered into with abandon or not at all.'

—

Harriet Van Horne

Lunchtime verrine

A layered salad in glass is known as a verrine in France. Traditionally small, they are designed to excite tiny appetites with their visual impact. This version in a jar is ready to transport for a healthy office lunch. The best bit of this salad for me is the broccoli stem. I'm hooked and now use it in so many dishes, and it means there is no waste. To shave the vegetables into ribbons, use a peeler or mandolin.

½ head broccoli, long stem left whole

4 asparagus spears, halved lengthways then sliced in half across

150g carrots, peeled, shaved into ribbons and finely shredded

50g piece of mooli, peeled, shaved into ribbons and finely shredded

1 celery stick, finely sliced diagonally, leaves reserved

a few sprigs of flat-leaf parsley, finely chopped

⅓ portion of cooked Puy lentils (page 121)

1 small red pepper, quartered, deseeded and skinned

5 pitted black olives, finely chopped

a few slices of smoked trout or salmon or shredded leftover chicken

⅓ portion of cooked *Quinoa* (page 130)

1 tablespoon sunflower seeds

2 tablespoons *Mustard and balsamic vinaigrette* (page 207)

Remove the small florets from the broccoli stem. Peel then slice the stem very thinly. Blanch the broccoli florets in a pan of salted boiling water for 30 seconds then lift out with a slotted spoon and transfer to a bowl of cold water. Blanch the stem slices for 20 seconds, lift out with a slotted spoon, refresh under cold running water and drain again. Transfer to a plate lined with kitchen paper. Drain the florets and pop them onto the plate with the stems and set aside.

Blanch the asparagus in the same water for 1 minute, drain, refresh under cold running water and put on a plate lined with kitchen paper.

Layer everything up in a large, wide jar with a lid. Mix the carrot, mooli and celery together and put in the bottom of the jar with the asparagus on top. Mix the parsley into the lentils and spoon onto the asparagus.

Put the broccoli florets in a mini processor, blitz to a grainy texture and tip into a bowl. Cut the pepper into fine dice and add to the broccoli with the chopped olives. Spoon some onto the lentils followed by the smoked trout and lay the sliced broccoli stems on top. Mix the quinoa with the sunflower seeds and add to the jar. Finally, top with the celery leaves. Put the dressing in a separate jar and when ready to eat, pour it onto the salad, give it a shake, then tip into a bowl or just eat from the jar.

WASTE NOT

The broccoli, red pepper and olive mixture can be added to *Ali's quick fix of ravioli, courgette and goat's cheese* (page 64) instead of the courgette. Just add it when the pasta has been cooked and drained.

Saffron pasta 'rags'

Look for an Italian brand of 'oo' flour, the best there is for pasta making. To get a wildly pink pasta, use 1 teaspoon of sifted beetroot powder (available in health and wholefood stores and online) in place of the saffron in the recipe below. Or to get a flecked green pasta, use two teaspoons of *Curly kale ash* (page 204). Make whatever shapes you like but I find the imperfection of the rags just perfect.

MAKES ABOUT 350G

¼ teaspoon saffron strands

2 medium eggs

200g Italian 'oo' flour

fine polenta or extra Italian 'oo' flour, to dust

Crush the saffron strands using a pestle and mortar, add the eggs and mix well. Put the flour in a food processor, pour in the egg mixture then pulse until the mixture forms couscous-style grains.

Tip onto the work surface (not marble, it's too cold) and knead until smooth. Flatten a little and wrap in clingfilm and chill for 1 hour to relax the gluten, which makes it easier to stretch. You can leave it overnight if you wish.

If you have a pasta machine, roll out about a quarter of the dough at a time, otherwise roll out as thinly as you can get it. If the dough is sticking to the work surface, dust with a little extra polenta or flour. Tear into long rags and freeze on a tray in a single layer. Once frozen hard, carefully pile into a container and freeze. You can then cook as many as you like from frozen. To cook from frozen, add to a large pan of salted boiling water and cook for 2–3 minutes until al dente (or follow any recipe instructions). Drain and serve.

WASTE NOT

You can use this pasta for the *Pasta rags with mackerel* on page 63 or cook it and serve with *Rich tomato sauce* (page 127). Once hot, add a can of drained tuna and fold in some spinach leaves for a swift supper.

Red rice with saba

For use in the *Crispy sausage, red rice, romanesco and pomegranate* (page 45) or use as an accompaniment to the *Cod fillet with rainbow chard and sobrasada* (page 59).

Use this method for cooking black rice as well, it needs only 5 minutes soaking time but another 5 minutes added to the cooking time. Leave out the oil and saba for black rice. Once cold, both red and black rice will keep in the fridge for up to three days and can be used as a vehicle for lots of flavours to accompany meat, fish or vegetables. To reheat, simply put a portion in a bowl and heat in a steamer until really hot.

MAKES ABOUT 2 PORTIONS

125g red camargue rice

2 teaspoons olive oil

1 tablespoon saba or vincotta

sea salt crystals

Soak the rice in a sieve set in a bowl of cold water for about 15 minutes. Rinse under cold water and drain.

Put the oil and rice in a medium pan with 350ml cold water. Bring to the boil, reduce the heat and half-cover the pan and cook for 10 minutes.

Cover completely and cook for 10–15 minutes. When just tender, add a pinch of salt and the saba, turn off the heat and leave on the hob covered for about 15 minutes to absorb any liquid that is left in the pan.

Puy lentils

Use in *Lunchtime verrine* (page 118) or *Agrodolce onions* (page 123) with merguez or for *Prawn, cod and courgette fritters* (page 98).

MAKES 2–3 SERVINGS

125g Puy lentils

pinch of sea salt crystals

2 tablespoons olive oil

Soak the lentils in cold water for 10 minutes. Drain and put in a pan and cover with cold water by about 2cm. Bring to the boil then reduce the heat, half-cover the pan and simmer for 15–20 minutes, until just tender. Remove from the heat, add the salt, cover and leave to sit for 5 minutes. Drain and add the oil and allow to cool completely. The lentils will keep for up to two days covered in the fridge.

Agrodolce onions

These are even tastier the following day as the sweet and sour sauce seeps into the onions a little more. A strong Cheddar-style cheese along with a hunk of bread and an assortment of charcuterie go well with the onions too.

You could use small shallots or onions in place of the jumbo salad onions (often known as continental onions) for this recipe. When making the *Pea and lemon risotto with shimeji mushrooms and burrata* (page 170) I reserve the fat white bulbs from the salad onions to use in this recipe – waste not want not!

MAKES ABOUT 4 SERVINGS

4 tablespoons caster sugar

4 tablespoons white balsamic vinegar

1 tablespoon olive oil

white bulbs from 2 bunches of jumbo salad onions, broken into lobes or 2 handfuls of shallots or tiny onions

1 tablespoon extra virgin olive oil

2 tablespoons capers, drained if brined or rinsed if salted

2 tablespoons *Toasted pine nuts* (page 200)

a small handful of flat-leaf parsley leaves, roughly chopped

Put the sugar and 2 teaspoons of water in a medium pan over a low heat and watch until the sugar starts to caramelise around the edges of the pan. Give the pan a gentle swirl and continue to cook until it is an even golden caramel colour, then immediately remove from the heat. Put on your oven gloves, stand back, then add the vinegar – the mixture will splatter a lot so be careful! Set aside.

Heat the olive oil in a frying pan and add the onions, fry over a low heat for about 8 minutes, turning occasionally until golden in parts and almost cooked through.

Use a slotted spoon to lift the onions out of the oil and add them to the agrodolce mixture in the saucepan along with 1 tablespoon of water. Cover with a cartouche (a circle of baking parchment cut to the size of the pan) – lay it on top of the onions – then cover the pan with a lid and continue to cook over a low heat for 5–10 minutes depending on their size. Add the extra virgin olive oil and stir for 1 minute or until the liquid has thickened a little and the onions are tender. Fold in the capers, pine nuts and parsley and remove from the heat. Eat right away or store in a bowl in the fridge for up to a week.

WASTE NOT

Serve Agrodolce onions with ½ portion of *Puy lentils* (page 121), some cooked merguez sausages and chard leaves with china rose radish sprouts (found in wholefood and health shops).

Basmati rice

Fill a measuring jug with white basmati rice up to the 100ml mark, tip into a sieve and rinse with cold running water until the water runs clear. Put in a small pan with 200ml cold water and a small pinch of sea salt crystals and bring to the boil. Reduce the heat – using a heat diffuser mat helps – cover and cook for 15 minutes. Remove from the heat and leave to stand, with the lid on, for 10 minutes. Use a fork to fluff up the rice and serve.

To reheat, put a portion in a bowl that will fit into a pan on a collpasible wire basket. Put a few centimetres of cold water in the pan first. Cover the pan with a lid and steam the rice over a medium heat until the lid rattles then reduce the heat right down until the rice is very hot and separates nicely when prodded with a fork

Roasted butternut squash & pumpkin

If you feel, as I do, that it's too much trouble to peel squash or pumpkin, I just eat if off the skin or scoop off the flesh if using as part of a salad.

MAKES 2 SERVINGS

1 small butternut squash or ½ medium pumpkin or 1 small pumpkin

a few sprigs of thyme

1 tablespoon olive or rapeseed oil

freshly ground black pepper

Deseed the squash or pumpkin and slice into thick wedges (I don't bother to peel off the skin but feel free to). Grind over some black pepper, scatter over the thyme sprigs, spoon over the oil and roast for 45–55 minutes. Serve as an accompaniment to all kinds of roasts or use in *Pumpkin and cavolo nero with soft goat's cheese and polpetti* (page 90).

Rich tomato sauce

This may seem like a lot of olive oil but it cooks down with the tomatoes to form a rich sauce. Add a big splash of extra virgin olive oil at the end for extra richness. You'll need to peel the tomatoes but, I think it's crucial how, just follow the instructions below. For smart occasions you could deseed the tomatoes after peeling but I like to leave them in for extra fibre, unless the tomatoes are very seedy. Then I chop the tomatoes into quarters and squeeze the seeds into a sieve set over a bowl, using a ladle to squash through all the jelly goodness into the juice below.

500g ripe tomatoes

4 tablespoons olive oil

3 garlic cloves, crushed to a paste with a large pinch of salt or 3 teaspoons *Crushed garlic* (page 207)

¾ teaspoon freshly ground black pepper

2 tablespoons extra virgin olive oil (optional)

First, peel the tomatoes. Use a sharp knife to cut a criss-cross at the bottom of each tomato and cover with boiling water from the kettle. Leave for no longer than 40 seconds, otherwise the skin comes off too thickly, taking some of the colour and flavour with it. Peel the skin, deseed if desired and chop the flesh roughly.

Set a pan over a medium heat and add the oil and garlic. Heat, stirring a little, until it fizzes and separates – without browning – then remove from the heat and add the chopped tomatoes. Instantly return to the heat, add the pepper and cook over a medium–high heat for no more than 12 minutes or until it thickens nicely. For the last 4 minutes, stir and reduce the heat if the sauce begins to catch on the bottom of the pan. Remove from the heat and, if using, stir in the extra virgin olive oil.

Pickled cucumber with dill labneh

If you can find the small Lebanese cucumbers often sold in Middle Eastern shops, and some supermarkets now, try them in this recipe as they have a great taste and really keep their crunch even after a few days' pickling. Eat the pickled cucumber and labneh with freshly cooked, lightly smoked salmon fillet (perhaps the fish left over from the *Runner bean, new potato, courgette and lightly smoked salmon salad* on page 110) along with tiny new potatoes. Labneh is a Middle Eastern-style strained yogurt and here it is beautifully flavoured with dill. It couldn't be easier to make.

2–3 small Lebanese cucumbers

1 tablespoon sea salt crystals

1 teaspoon caster sugar

3 tablespoons white balsamic vinegar

FOR THE DILL LABNEH

120g full-fat natural bio live yogurt

pinch of sea salt

a few sprigs of dill, chopped

a few borage flowers (optional), to serve

pinch of sumac, to sprinkle

First make the labneh. Scoop the yogurt into a small nylon sieve set over a bowl, cover and put in the fridge to drain for about 3 hours or overnight. Tip into a bowl and season with a pinch of salt and mix in the dill. Add borage flowers if you have them and sprinkle with sumac.

To pickle the cucumbers, groove their skin (because it looks beautiful) with a canelle knife or peel in strips with a vegetable peeler and slice the cucumbers into 3mm rounds. Put into a dish and toss with the salt and set aside for 30 minutes. Put the sugar and vinegar into a bowl and stir well to dissolve. Lightly rinse the cucumber slices and add to the vinegar mixture. Layer up in a jar and keep in the fridge to use within a few weeks.

Freekeh

This delicious young, green and toasted wheat is chock full of goodness with a low GI and has the ability to soak up all sorts of flavourful additions. Depending on the brand you buy you may need to clean the freekeh. Just tip it onto a tray and take a minute to check the grains and carefully fish out any pieces of grit.

MAKES ABOUT 2–3 PORTIONS

100g freekeh

2 teaspoons olive oil

½ teaspoon organic vegetable bouillon powder

pinch of sea salt crystals

Wash and rinse the freekeh and leave to drain for 20 minutes or so until the grains are surface dried. Preheat the oven to 180°C/gas mark 4.

Heat the oil in an ovenproof pan over a low heat and add the freekeh, stir to coat in oil. Stir in the bouillon powder and 250ml boiling water and bring to a simmer. Cover with a lid or foil and bake for 25 minutes until the water is absorbed and the grains are soft. Remove from the oven.

Stir in a little salt and leave to sit, covered, for about 20 minutes then fork through the grains to make them nice and fluffy. Use straightaway or leave until completely cold, then store in the fridge for up to three days.

WASTE NOT

For more with freekeh see *Black pudding, caramelised persimmon and freekeh with raspberry salad cream* (page 42).

Quinoa

All wholefood stores sell this nutritious grain in a range of colours but it's fun to mix your own assortment. Quinoa is excellent in salads and can be used in *Lunchtime verrine* (page 118) or *Roasted cauliflower, fennel and chorizo puchero with quinoa* (page 93). It will keep in the fridge for up to four days.

MAKES ENOUGH FOR 2–3 SERVINGS

75g white, red, purple or tricolore quinoa

pinch of sea salt crystals

Rinse the quinoa in cold water, drain in a sieve, put in a small pan and cover with cold water by just under a centimetre. Bring to the boil, cover, reduce the heat and simmer for 15 minutes. Add the salt, stir, remove from the heat and leave to sit, covered, for 10 minutes or until the liquid has been fully absorbed.

Polenta –
soft & griddled

Polenta is great served soft and wet, as soon as it is made, with a meaty casserole. The remaining portion can be set in a tin and griddled or fried another day. If you prefer, you can leave out the Parmesan.

90g good-quality Italian instant polenta

3 tablespoons extra virgin olive oil

40g Parmesan, freshly and finely grated (optional)

olive oil, for greasing (see below)

sea salt crystals and freshly ground black pepper

Rinse an 18cm square, 4cm deep tin with cold water (this prevents the polenta from sticking – there is no need for oil).

Put 725ml cold water in a saucepan and bring to the boil over a medium heat, whisking to stop it boiling over. Pour in all the polenta at once, whisking like mad to stop lumps from forming, while maintaining a simmer for 1 minute.

Reduce the heat and whisk for 3–4 minutes until the mixture begins to leave the sides of the pan. Add the oil, and if using, stir in the Parmesan and season to taste. Spoon a portion into a bowl if eating when hot and soft right away. Spoon the remainder into the dampened tin and use a spatula dipped in water to smooth over the surface.

FOR GRIDDLED POLENTA

Once the polenta has completely cooled, tip onto a board and cut into the shapes you want. Put onto a plate or tray lined with baking parchment and leave, uncovered, in the fridge for at least 30 minutes or up to three days to dry out, otherwise it might stick when griddling.

To cook, brush the surface of the polenta with oil and heat a griddle pan or a frying pan over a high heat. Griddle the polenta for about 2 minutes on each side or until golden to your liking.

'One cannot think well, love
well or sleep well if one has
not dined well.'

—

Virginia Woolf

A MEZZE MEAL

Make as many of these recipes as you fancy to have for a snack meal or as accompaniments to other recipes. To go with the mezze assortment, put out a tiny bowl of rapeseed mayo, some pink salt with finely grated lemon zest and lemon wedges.

A bowl of onion & coriander with a touch of chilli

¾ pink shallot or red onion or onion, finely sliced

juice of ½ lemon

a hank of coriander, leaves removed

1 mild red chilli, deseeded and roughly chopped

Mix together the shallot and lemon juice in a small bowl. Set aside for 5–10 minutes (the lemon juice will make the shallot a glorious pink colour).

Toss in the coriander leaves and sprinkle with chopped chilli.

Coconut pancakes

Like all pancake-making you get into a rhythm, and before you know it you have a perfect pile.

The batter does benefit from resting in the fridge – make it a couple hours or up to a day before you want to cook the pancakes.

MAKES 10 PANCAKES OR MORE IF USING A SMALL FRYING PAN

4 tablespoons coconut flour

1 tablespoon white spelt flour

⅛ teaspoon bicarbonate of soda

¼ teaspoon cream of tartar

3 small eggs

125ml coconut milk

sunflower oil, for frying

Put the flours, bicarbonate of soda and cream of tartar in a bowl and whisk in the eggs and the coconut milk until smooth. Allow the mixture to rest for at least 2 hours or overnight in the fridge.

Whisk in 7–8 tablespoons of cold water (you may not need all of it if the coconut milk you use is very runny) to get the consistency of thin cream. Heat a 20cm (preferably non-stick) frying pan over a high heat to get it nice and hot then reduce the heat to the lowest setting. Have a bowl of oil handy and wipe out the pan with a wad of kitchen paper dipped in the oil. Add a small ladleful of batter and swirl the pan to spread the batter evenly and to get a nice wavy edge. Cook for 2–3 minutes until the base is golden. Use a spatula to carefully flip it over and cook the other side for about 1½ minutes or until cooked to your liking. Continue to cook the remaining pancakes until all the mixture is used.

Split pea hummus with black olives & crispy capers

Cook the full 100g of split peas, this way it will also give you enough for the *Shami kebabs* (page 146). Prepare the split peas the night before you want to eat this dish.

100g yellow split peas (chana dal)

pinch of sea salt crystals

2 tablespoons organic tahini

1 garlic clove crushed to a paste with a little salt or 1 teaspoon *Crushed garlic* (page 207)

2–3 tablespoons extra virgin olive oil

juice of ½–1 lemon

scattering of Crispy capers (page 202)

a few small black olives

Soak the split peas in cold water overnight.

Drain the split peas, put in a pan and cover with cold water by a few centimetres. Slowly bring to the boil and skim off any froth that develops on the surface. Reduce the heat and gently simmer for about 30 minutes or until tender. Remove from the heat, add salt and leave, covered, for 10 minutes. Drain and set aside to cool completely, until ready to use half for this recipe. Cover the remaining half and store in the fridge or freezer.

Put the split peas in a mini food processor with the tahini, garlic, 1 tablespoon of the oil and half the lemon juice and whizz to a purée. You may need a little cold water to get a soft, creamy consistency — but taste before adding any extra lemon juice. Tip into a serving bowl and top with the remaining oil, crispy capers and black olives.

Chickpeas in tomato sauce with feta & parsley

I find that canned chickpeas are easier to digest and have more of a home-cooked flavour if they are drained, rinsed well and briefly cooked again in fresh water before draining.

200g (½ large can) chickpeas, drained and rinsed

½ portion of *Rich tomato sauce* (page 127)

a small handful flat-leaf parsley leaves, chopped

100g feta

Cook the drained chickpeas in salted boiling water for 5 minutes and drain.

Heat the Rich tomato sauce in a small pan over a medium heat. Add the chickpeas and cook together for 4 minutes to warm through. Tip into a bowl and scatter with the parsley and crumble over the feta.

WASTE NOT

Any leftover chickpeas can be used in the *Goan fish curry* (page 107). To use up any feta, see *Farro with spinach, feta and olives* (page 84).

Beetroot crane

2 medium beetroot, unpeeled

¼ pink shallot or red onion, finely sliced
   then halved

juice of ½ lemon

2 tablespoons hot horseradish sauce

1 tablespoon natural yogurt

a few leaves of micro radish sprouts
   (or chopped dill)

Cook the beetroot in a pan of salted boiling water for 40 minutes or until tender. Drain and run them briefly under cold running water. Then fill the pan with water and rub off the peel under water – this avoids the 'carnage-in-the-kitchen' look! (Don't worry about your hands, the colour will wash off.) Chop into small dice and put into a bowl.

Mix the shallot with the lemon juice in a small bowl and set aside.

Mix the horseradish sauce and yogurt in another bowl and fold this lightly through the beetroot. Top with some of the shallot (leaving the juice behind) and micro leaves and fold all together.

WASTE NOT

Any spare raw beetroot can be used in my *Chocolate, beetroot and orange torte* (page 160). Spare pink shallot or onion can be used in *A bowl of onion and coriander with a touch of chilli* (page 134).

Hünkar beğendi

'The sultan enjoyed it' is the rough translation for hünkar beğendi – and you will too! Turkish in origin, my version of this aubergine dish is a little lighter and over the years has been a great success as part of a cross-cultural mezze or small plates tuck-in.

1 medium aubergine (about 350g)

2–3 tablespoons olive oil

juice of ½ lemon

20g Parmesan or pecorino

1 tablespoon extra virgin olive oil

a few pinches of pul biber pepper flakes

sea salt crystals

Preheat the grill to high and arrange the rack about 15cm away from the heat.

Line a large oven tray with foil. Slice the aubergine into rounds a little less than 1cm wide and toss with the olive oil on the oven tray and separate out into a single layer. Grill the aubergine slices for 4 minutes on each side then raise the rack closer to the heat and grill for about 2 minutes on each side or until they become golden and slightly charred in parts (keep a close watch).

Season the aubergine slices lightly with salt then tip into a bowl. Use a pair of kitchen scissors to snip the aubergine into chunky, randomly sized pieces. Stir in the lemon juice. With a vegetable peeler, shave the Parmesan over the aubergine, spoon over the extra virgin olive oil and top with the pul biber.

WASTE NOT

This dish is used in the *Charred ciabatta with smoky steak, courgettes and aubergine* (page 33).

Raw dressed courgettes with pine nuts

1 pale green Lebanese, yellow or green courgette

1 tablespoon or more of *Mustard and white balsamic vinaigrette* (page 207)

a scattering of *Toasted pine nuts* (page 200)

pinch of Espelette pepper

Thinly slice the courgette, put in a bowl and spoon over the dressing. Scatter over the toasted pine nuts and sprinkle with Espelette pepper.

WASTE NOT

Any spare courgettes are delicious simply grilled. Slice the courgettes, toss them in a little good olive oil and top with a scattering of pul biber or Espelette pepper. Spread on a foil-lined baking tray and grill, on a rack set about 15cm from the heat, for about 12 minutes turning halfway through or until lightly charred in places.

Runner beans with smoked salmon

5 or more runner beans, thinly sliced diagonally

2 teaspoons *Mustard and white balsamic vinaigrette* (page 207)

a few slices of smoked salmon, torn into shreds

a few scoops of salmon or trout roe (optional)

Cook the runner beans in a small pan of boiling salted water for 3 minutes. Drain and refresh under cold running water, then drain again and transfer to a bowl. Toss in the vinaigrette, add the salmon and a few scoops of salmon roe, if using.

Lovage-scented pork cheeks with cider, prunes & kale

Lovage is a perennial herb, which is so easy to grow and gets very tall mid-summer, so just chop it down to about 10cm and it will keep going until winter. It's great tossed with lentils too. If lovage isn't available, juniper berries will also work. Look for purple variegated kale at farmers' markets or use easily available green kale.

As soon as you get the pork home, unwrap it and put in a shallow container with 1 tablespoon of rapeseed oil rubbed over, cover and keep in the fridge until the next day if you need to. You should get a few meals from this or freeze what's left once cooled completely. Pork cheeks cook down to a tender piece of joy but feel free to use two pork shoulder chops for a change. I also love this cooked with Pedro Ximenez sherry instead of cider.

MAKES ENOUGH FOR 2 SERVINGS

400g pig cheeks, skinned

2 tablespoons rapeseed oil

12 small shallots, peeled

2 garlic cloves crushed to a paste with a little sea salt or 2 teaspoons *Crushed garlic* (page 207)

8 pitted prunes

2 sprigs of fresh lovage (or 5 juniper berries, lightly crushed)

150ml strong and slightly sweet organic cider

a handful of curly kale, tough stems discarded and leaves torn

sea salt crystals and freshly ground black pepper

soft or griddled polenta (page 131) or a baked sweet potato, to serve

Preheat the oven to 190°C/gas mark 5. Cut each cheek in half, season well and set aside.

Heat half the oil in a heavy ovenproof casserole over a medium–high heat and fry the shallots for about 5 minutes until tinged golden, lift onto a plate using a slotted spoon. Add the remaining oil and sear the pork on both sides until golden. Add the garlic, shallots, prunes and lovage, pour over the cider and bring almost to the boil.

Cover with a cartouche (a circle of baking parchment cut to the size of the pan) – lay it on top of the pork – then cover the casserole with a lid and cook in the oven for 10 minutes. Reduce the oven temperature to 160°C/gas mark 3 and cook for a further 1 hour. Remove and check the pork is done; it should be very tender and the connective tissue should have broken down. Remove the lovage stems and throw in the torn kale and pop back in the oven for a further 10 minutes. Remove from the oven and leave to rest for 10 minutes before serving.

Bulgogi beef with sigumchi namul & quick kimchi

I first ate this, many years ago, in a Korean restaurant located in the basement of a smart Hong Kong hotel. Each table was kitted out with its own extractor fan as you had to grill the beef yourself. If you have a small camping stove use a ridged griddle pan and grill the beef in the open air. The sigumchi namul is such a tasty and versatile side dish – try it with seared scallops or a piece of baked fish.

40g jasmine rice

pinch of sea salt crystals

1 portion of *Quick kimchi* (page 204)

FOR THE BULGOGI BEEF

1 teaspoon coconut palm sugar

1 tablespoon light soy sauce

2 teaspoons sesame oil

1 garlic clove, sliced and crushed to a paste with a pinch of salt or 1 teaspoon *Crushed garlic* (page 207)

pinch of freshly ground black pepper

175–200g piece prime fillet steak, cut into 1cm slices

FOR THE SIGUMCHI NAMUL

150g spinach

1 teaspoon sesame oil

1 tablespoon light soy sauce

2 teaspoons mirin

½ teaspoon *Toasted sesame seeds* (page 200)

To make the bulgogi, mix the marinade ingredients together in a non-corrosive container just big enough to fit the meat in a single layer and add the meat. Cover and put in the fridge overnight or for at least 3 hours.

To make the sigumchi namul, put the spinach in a large pan over a medium heat and pour over a little boiling water. Cover and leave for 1 minute until just wilted. Drain and refresh under cold running water and squeeze out as much of the liquid as possible. Mix the sesame oil, soy sauce and mirin in a non-corrosive bowl and roughly chop the spinach and stir into the bowl. Scatter with toasted sesame seeds, cover and chill until needed.

Half an hour before you want to eat, cook the rice. Rinse the rice well and put in a small saucepan and just cover with boiling water. Add a pinch of salt and cover and cook for 15 minutes. Leave to rest off the heat, covered, for 10 minutes. A heat diffuser mat is useful when cooking the perfect pan of rice.

Heat a griddle pan over a high heat until a few drops of water sprinkled on the surface evaporate instantly. Flash-fry the meat in batches for 15–30 seconds on each side. Serve while hot with the sigumchi namul, rice and some kimchi on the side.

Red-cooked pork belly with choy sum

Black beans are salted fermented soybeans and give a distinctive tang to this dish; they last a long time stored in an airtight jar. Buy a good rare-breed piece of belly pork with a healthy layer of fat and a nice dry skin after cooking. The pork fat will rise to the top when chilled, leaving a jelly below. Good pork fat and jelly is a treat on bread or cold toast with pepper.

FOR THE RED-COOKED BELLY PORK

2 teaspoons sesame oil

1 tablespoon coconut palm sugar

3 tablespoons light soy sauce

100g banana shallot, finely sliced

3 garlic cloves, thinly sliced

1cm piece of fresh ginger, peeled and sliced

2 lemongrass stems, split lengthways and bruised

¼ teaspoon ground star anise

1 teaspoon ground Sichuan pepper

1 long red chilli, deseeded (if you prefer) and finely chopped

1 x 700g boneless belly pork with skin

FOR THE CHOY SUM

1 bunch choy sum

1 garlic clove, crushed with a little salt or 1 teaspoon *Crushed garlic* (page 207)

3 spring onions, thinly sliced

2 teaspoons Chinese salted black beans, roughly chopped

1 teaspoon light soy sauce

pinch of coconut palm sugar

Preheat the oven to 200°C/gas mark 6. Put all the ingredients for the pork in a heavy lidded casserole with 2 tablespoons of water and rub the meat all over with the mixture. Take off any solid ingredients left on the skin, cover and bake for 20 minutes. Reduce the oven temperature to 160°C/gas mark 3 and cook for a further 1 hour 15 minutes.

Remove from the oven. Take the lid off the casserole, add 4 tablespoons of water and use a sharp knife to score the skin; there is no need to take the pork out of the casserole as it cuts like butter. Cook for a further 30 minutes then lift out onto a warmed plate. Strain the sauce into a bowl and remove any you don't want to use right away to a small container and transfer to the fridge once cold. (It will turn to jelly.) Put the meat back into the casserole.

If you like crackling, preheat the grill to its highest setting. Put the meat under the grill until you have nice bubbly, crunchy crackling. Remove and set aside to rest for 20 minutes.

To prepare the choy sum, slice up into the stem end and set aside. Put the remaining ingredients with 1 tablespoon water in a wok set over a high heat and when hot add the choy sum, cover and reduce the heat to low and steam for 2–3 minutes or until the stems are tender. Baste occasionally, adding a little water if it becomes too dry.

To serve, slice the meat thickly and place on a warmed plate with some of the cooking liquid spooned over and the choy sum alongside.

WASTE NOT

Any leftover pork and jelly can be used in the filling for the *Pork and kimchi gyozas with sweet tare* (page 144).

Pork & kimchi gyoza with sweet tare

These tasty morsels use up excess ingredients from the *Red-cooked pork belly with choy sum* (page 142) and *Quick kimchi* (page 204); both having been made in advance. The making of gyozas is a good rainy weekend activity. The sweet soy dipping sauce or tare keeps in the fridge for up to a week but it's quick and easy to make another batch if need be. These are also delicious served with pak choi, chilli and ginger (see page 56).

MAKES 20–25 GYOZAS

150g *Red-cooked pork belly*, sliced and chopped into small pieces (page 142)

4 teaspoons firm jelly from the *Red-cooked pork belly* (page 142)

140g *Quick kimchi*, drained and chopped (page 204)

15g chives

20 gyoza wrappers (available from Asian food shops)

1 tablespoon sunflower oil

FOR THE SWEET TARE

4 tablespoons tamari or light soy sauce

4 tablespoons mirin

5 teaspoons coconut palm sugar or brown sugar

TO SERVE

2–3 spring onions

8cm piece of cucumber

Put the pork, jelly and kimchi in a bowl and snip in the chives. Mix well. Have the pile of gyoza wrappers at the ready, along with a small bowl of water. Line a tray with clingfilm that is large enough to fit all the gyozas in a single layer and sit easily in the freezer until they freeze hard (then you can transfer them to a smaller container).

Take a wrapper in one hand and dip a finger into the water and wet the rim of the wrapper. Put just a little more than a teaspoon of pork mixture in the centre. Fold over to make a half moon but stop it sticking until you have pleated one side from the centre on to the back side of the wrapper then repeat from the centre again on to the other side until you have a curved crescent shape pleated on one side only. Lay them side by side on the lined tray and freeze for 4 hours or overnight.

For the sweet tare, put the ingredients in a small pan over a low heat for 2 minutes, swirling the pan to help dissolve the sugar. Increase the heat slightly and simmer for about 4 minutes until reduced to a syrup. Pour into a small serving bowl for dipping.

To prepare the serving ingredients, first trim and cut the spring onions into lengths then shred thinly lengthways and put into a bowl of cold water to curl. Cut the cucumber in half lengthways and into two across. Remove the seeds with a spoon, slice into matchstick pieces and put in a serving bowl.

When ready to eat, put a frying pan over a medium–high heat and add the oil and as many gyozas from the freezer as you want to eat. Fry them on one side for 1–2 minutes until just golden, gently turn them and fry the other side for a further 1–2 minutes. Carefully add 75ml water (it will spit), immediately cover with a lid and reduce the heat to a gentle simmer and steam for 2–3 minutes or until the water has just evaporated and they are heated through.

Drain the spring onions, pat them dry with kitchen paper and mix with the cucumber. Serve scattered over the gyozas along with the sweet tare dipping sauce and pak choi, chilli and ginger if using.

Shami kebabs

This dish is a reminder of my earliest introductions to Indian cooking. Traditionally, the kebabs are stuffed with raw onion but I prefer to have my raw onions in a *Kachumber* (page 216) and serve that alongside the kebabs. The roast lamb meat really does benefit from a few hours marinating in the spices so try to make this at least a few hours before (or overnight). The magic of this recipe is that it can provide two meals: the roasted lamb fillet that you can eat a small piece of right away, and the rest cooked further in the spices below.

MAKES 10

FOR THE SHAMI

100g yellow split peas (chana dal)

2 lamb neck fillets (about 500g), at room temperature

1 tablespoon olive oil

1cm piece of fresh ginger, peeled and finely grated

3 garlic cloves, finely chopped

finely grated zest of ½ lemon

½ teaspoon ground cumin

1½ teaspoons ground coriander

¼ teaspoon ground turmeric

½ teaspoon chilli powder

¼ teaspoon freshly ground black pepper

2 teaspoons potato flour

1 egg yolk

10g coriander leaves, finely chopped

1 tablespoon sunflower oil, for frying

sea salt crystals and freshly ground black pepper

TO SERVE

1 lime, cut into wedges

½ portion *Kachumber* (page 216)

Indian flatbreads (optional)

Put the split peas in a small pan and cover with cold water by 2cm. Bring just to the boil and when it froths reduce the heat to low and cook for about 1 hour or until very soft. Remove from the heat, add a pinch of salt and leave for 10 minutes. Drain well and leave until completely cool.

Preheat the oven to 200°C/gas mark 6. Put the lamb on a foil-lined baking tray and coat with the olive oil, season with salt and freshly ground black pepper. Roast for 45 minutes. Rest half of one fillet for 15 minutes and eat it sliced with vegetables of your choice.

Meanwhile, put the ginger, garlic, lemon zest and spices into a small ovenproof pot. Take the remaining lamb and cut into 2cm cubes and add to the spice mixture in the pot along with any juices and stir to coat. Cover with a cartouche (a circle of baking parchment cut to the size of the pot) – lay it on top of the lamb – then cover with a tight-fitting lid. Cook for 15 minutes then reduce the oven temperature to 160°C/gas mark 3. Continue to cook for a further 40 minutes until the meat has absorbed

the liquid. Leave to cool completely – I like to leave it overnight – then remove any hardened fat from around the meat.

To make the shami kebabs, put the lamb, half the cooked split peas (see Waste not), potato flour and egg yolk into a mini food processor and pulse to form a stiff, smooth paste. You may need to do this in two batches. Transfer to a bowl and add the chopped coriander, mixing it well with your hands. Mould into ten patties about 4cm in diameter and chill for 10 minutes. Heat the sunflower oil in a frying pan over a medium–high heat. Add the patties in two batches (don't overcrowd them otherwise they

steam) and fry them for about 3 minutes on each side until golden. Serve hot with the lime wedges, the Kachumber and a couple of flatbreads if you like.

WASTE NOT

Any leftover kebabs can be easily reheated. Simply wrap them in foil and place in a hot oven for 5 minutes. As you have cooked the full 100g split peas (chana dal) this way it will give you enough for the recipe for *Hummus* (page 135). Or you can freeze half the cooked split peas for another occasion.

Quail stuffed with maftoul & roasted in vine leaves

When you get your quail home unwrap it and rub with a dash of olive oil, put in a deep dish and cover with a double layer of baking parchment to stop it drying out. It will keep in the fridge like this if you want to wait for a day before you cook it. You can buy dried marigold petals in Chinese stores and online if you don't have fresh available.

2 quail, necks removed, at room temperature

2 tablespoons olive oil

50g maftoul, giant couscous or fregola sarda

1 tablespoon extra virgin olive oil

finely grated zest and juice of 1 lemon

2 tablespoons chopped chives

2 tablespoons pistachio nibs

½ teaspoon pul biber pepper flakes

petals from 2 marigold flower heads

4 fresh young vine leaves (optional)

sea salt crystals and freshly ground black pepper

watercress dressed simply with *Mustard and white balsamic vinaigrette* (page 207) or blanched spinach or chard, to serve

Preheat the oven to 200°C/gas mark 6.

Wipe the insides of the quails well with kitchen paper and season, inside and out, with a little salt and half the lemon juice.

Heat 1 tablespoon of the olive oil in a frying pan over a medium heat and stir-fry the maftoul for about 2 minutes until golden. Add 125ml cold water (be careful, it will splatter) and a little salt, and simmer for a few minutes until all the water is absorbed. Add another 100ml water, reduce the heat a little and continue to cook for 4 minutes. Remove from the heat, add the extra virgin olive oil and the remaining lemon juice, cover and set aside for 10 minutes.

Tip the maftoul into a bowl and cool completely. Add the lemon zest, chives, pistachios, pul biber and marigold petals.

Put the quails on a baking tray and stuff with as much of the maftoul stuffing as you can and tie the legs together loosely with kitchen string. Spoon over the remaining olive oil and season the skin. Tuck a vine leaf under each quail and also place one over the top. Roast for 25 minutes then remove from the oven and rest for 10 minutes. Snip the string around the legs and serve with a watercress salad or simply cooked spinach or chard.

Yuba lasagne with kale, squash, tomato & mozzarella

Yuba is paper-thin tofu (also known as bean curd skin). Fresh yuba is available from Asian supermarkets or online. When buying, make sure to check the packet for non-GMO soybean. What you have left from a packet of fresh yuba can easily be sliced into noodles and used in *The hungry person's chicken noodle soup* (page 179). Make the lasagne the day before and chill until 30 minutes before baking.

1 tablespoon olive oil, plus extra for greasing

100g kale leaves, torn from the tough stems

130g fresh yuba

150g *Rich tomato sauce* (page 127)

125g mozzarella ball, drained

6 wedges of *Roasted butternut squash and pumpkin* (page 124)

50g Parmesan, freshly and finely grated

Preheat the oven to 180°C/gas mark 4. Heat 1 teaspoon of the oil in a wok, add the kale and stir-fry for a minute then add a splash of water and cover and cook for 3 minutes until tender. Drain and set aside.

Blanch the yuba in a pan of salted boiling water for 30 seconds, drain, transfer to a plate and add the remaining oil. You will need an approx. 800ml pie dish or casserole dish about 5cm deep, greased with oil.

Put a quarter of the yuba in the dish with about a third of the tomato sauce smoothed over the top. Add half the kale and tear half the mozzarella over it. Add another layer of yuba and smooth over half of the remaining tomato sauce. Cut the skin off the squash or pumpkin, slice each wedge into three and arrange on top of the sauce. Dust over half the grated Parmesan. Top with another layer of yuba and sauce and add the remaining kale and mozzarella. Top with the final quarter of yuba and dust with the remaining Parmesan.

Cover with a sheet of oiled foil and bake for 20 minutes. After this time, remove the foil and bake for a further 15 minutes or until golden.

WASTE NOT

Use any remaining kale in the *Lovage-scented pork cheeks with cider, prunes and kale* recipe on page 140 or *Toasted sourdough with Vignotte, curly kale and mushrooms* (page 32).

Strata

Strata has become a thing of joyous experimentation. It's a sort of frittata meets bread and butter pudding and this version is right up my street as it contains things left over from other recipes so there is nothing wasted from the fridge.

I like to soak the bread in the mixture in the morning and come home at the end of the day to add the final touches and cook. Eat hot with green salad. There should be plenty of strata left for a snack lunch the next day.

4 medium eggs

60ml double cream

2–3 tablespoons milk (if needed)

1 slice of good-quality bread, cubed

60g curly kale, torn from the tough stems

100g cooked lightly smoked salmon (or use unsmoked) fillet

50g soft rindless goat's cheese

pinch of pul biber pepper flakes

freshly ground black pepper

2 teaspoons olive oil

a small knob of butter

Whisk the eggs, cream and 2 tablespoons of milk in a bowl until smooth. Add the bread and stir well. Cover and chill for at least 1 hour or overnight. Remove from the fridge just before using and add a little extra milk.

Put the kale in a saucepan and pour over boiling water, set over a high heat and wilt for 3 minutes, drain and refresh in cold water. Drain again and squeeze as much moisture out as possible and use kitchen paper to pat dry. Chop roughly.

Preheat the grill to high and put the rack about 15cm from the heat.

Add the kale to the egg mixture and flake in the cooked salmon. Add knobs of half the soft goat's cheese, season and fold together gently to mix.

Heat a small (17cm) frying pan over a medium heat (if it has a wooden or plastic handle wrap the handle in foil to protect it when you use the grill) and add the oil and butter. When sizzling, add the mixture. Dot the top with the remaining goat's cheese and scatter with the pul biber.

Cook for about 2 minutes until the edges are just starting to bubble and puff then put under the grill to cook through for about 4 minutes until the surface is golden and puffed. Keep an eye on it – if it overbrowns but is still runny when touched, cover with foil and continue to grill on a lower rack for a few more minutes..

Bhuna khichuri

There's nothing quite as comforting as a kedgeree, well unless it's a khichuri. This Bengali precursor to that British colonial dish translates appropriately as 'a bit of a mess'. I love this dish with an aubergine pickle (I like Patak's) or a good prawn balchou (Goan prawn pickle). The whole red lentils are in fact brown in colour and very small. You could remove some of the khichuri before adding the prawns and store in the fridge when cooled completely. Serve this a day later with boiled eggs and some cooked smoked haddock or cooked smoked salmon.

75g masoor dal (whole red lentils)

75g basmati rice

3 tablespoons sunflower oil

4 fresh curry leaves

¼ teaspoon brown mustard seeds

1 small pink Bombay onion or large banana shallot, finely chopped

2 garlic cloves crushed with a little salt or 2 teaspoons *Crushed garlic* (page 207)

2cm piece of fresh ginger, peeled and grated

2 tablespoons barberries, soaked in a bowl of water for 15 minutes

100g fresh prawns, shelled and tails left on

1 long green chilli, deseeded and finely chopped

a large handful of *Crispy shallots* (page 202)

10g coriander, leaves removed from stems

a few dried rose petals (optional)

lemon wedges, to serve

sea salt crystals and freshly ground black pepper

Put the lentils in a bowl and cover with water for 30 minutes.

Rinse the rice in a sieve with cold water until the water runs clear. Drain the rice and lentils well. Put 2 tablespoons of the oil in a medium pan over a medium heat. Add the curry leaves and mustard seeds and, when they pop, add the onion, garlic and ginger and sweat for 5 minutes over a low heat. Add the lentils and rice and stir to coat with the mixture.

Cover with 300ml cold water, bring to just under boiling point, reduce the heat right down, cover and cook for 25–30 minutes until all the water has been absorbed (a heat diffuser mat is useful to create an even heat). When cooked, remove from the heat, drain the barberries and stir them in, season with salt and pepper, cover and leave to rest for 5–10 minutes.

Meanwhile, season the prawns with salt and pepper. Heat the remaining oil in a frying pan, add the prawns and stir-fry for 4 minutes until they are cooked through (they should be pale pink in colour). Throw in the chilli and stir well then add to the rice and lentils. Scatter with half the crispy shallots and fluff the khichuri up with a fork.

Serve topped with coriander leaves, the remaining crispy shallots, and rose petals, if using. Squeeze over some lemon juice as you eat.

Cavolo nero &
chestnut gnocchi
with pecorino nero

Chestnut paired with cavolo nero is a great match. However this recipe will be just as delicious made with curly kale. Find chestnuts ready cooked in vacuum packs; easy to use and very tasty.

Pecorino nero is a semi-hard sheep's milk cheese, which would have traditionally been rubbed with ash and olive skins to turn it the black colour of its name.

MAKES ABOUT 20 GNOCCHI

500g or 6 small potatoes (fluffy variety such as King Edward)

100g cavolo nero

2 teaspoons, plus 2 tablespoons olive oil

½ teaspoon *Crushed garlic* (page 207)

5 ready-cooked, vacuum-packed chestnuts

40g pecorino nero, plus extra for serving

finely grated zest of ½ lemon

2 large egg yolks

45g chestnut flour, plus extra to dust

extra virgin olive oil, for serving

saba or vincotto, to spoon over (optional)

sea salt crystals and freshly ground black pepper

Preheat the oven to 190°C/gas mark 5. Prick the potato skins a few times with a skewer and put on a baking tray and bake in the oven for 1 hour until soft and just golden.

Meanwhile, strip the fleshy leaves from the stems of the cavolo nero – you should have about 50g. Heat 2 teaspoons of the olive oil in a wok over a medium heat, add the garlic and the cavolo nero with 2 tablespoons of water. Cover and steam for 4 minutes. Drain – the garlic will cling where it wants – and when cool enough to handle, squeeze the leaves to remove all moisture then finely chop. Transfer to a plate lined with kitchen paper to drain further.

While the potatoes are still hot, cut them in half. Using a spoon, scoop the flesh into a sieve set over a bowl – you should have about 200g potato flesh. Using a ladle in a circular motion, push all the potato through the sieve (or use a potato ricer). Finely grate four of the chestnuts, the pecorino nero and the lemon zest into the potato. Add about 25g chopped cavolo nero (keep back the rest for serving), the egg yolks, chestnut flour and season with salt and pepper. Lightly mix with your hands to bring the mixture together.

Bring a pan of salted boiling water to a fast boil (use from the kettle for speed). Dust a clean surface with chestnut flour and divide the gnocchi mixture into

four. Roll out a portion at a time into a long sausage about 14cm long and snip into five pieces with scissors. Add them to the boiling water and cook for 3–4 minutes until they float to the surface. Scoop out with a slotted spoon onto a tray lined with kitchen paper. Repeat with the remaining portions of gnocchi.

At this point, take what you don't want to eat that day and put in a single layer in a container and add a spoon or so of olive oil (to prevent sticking). When cold, cover and put in the fridge. (Or freeze for no longer than a week. remove from the freezer 30 minutes before cooking.)

Heat 2 tablespoons of oil in a frying pan over a medium–high heat. Fry the gnocchi on each side until golden, about 3–4 minutes. Serve with the leftover chopped cavolo nero scattered over, extra pecorino nero and the single chestnut grated over the top. Spoon over a little extra virgin olive oil, saba, if using, grind over some black pepper and serve.

WASTE NOT

Any leftover chestnuts can be used in the quick fix *Chestnut and chocolate parfait* on page 79 or add some to the *Lovage-scented pork cheeks with cider, prunes and kale* on page 140.

Greengage & almond eve's pudding

Cooked greengages are lovely with porridge for breakfast with natural date syrup spooned over and the quantity here gives a few extra to use another day. If you don't have two pudding dishes the same size you could make this in one larger pudding dish. You could use apricots instead of greengages if out of season.

MAKES 2 SERVINGS

400g greengages, halved and stoned

40g caster sugar, plus 2 teaspoons for the greengages and a little to dust

50g salted butter, softened at room temperature

1 medium egg

25g self-raising flour

25g ground almonds

clotted cream or vanilla ice cream, to serve

Preheat the oven to 180°C/gas mark 4.

Put the greengages in a saucepan with 3 tablespoons of water and the 2 teaspoons of sugar and cover with a lid. Cook over a very low heat for 8–10 minutes until soft. Spoon a good layer of greengages evenly into two 5cm deep, 250ml capacity ovenproof dishes and leave to cool completely.

Put the remaining sugar and butter in a bowl and cream together with a wooden spoon or electric hand-held beater until soft and pale. Add the egg and beat to mix. Sift the flour and ground almonds in a bowl, then sift again, in two batches, over the egg mixture (add any extra ground almonds caught in the sieve). Fold in very gently to keep the volume.

Tip the mixture onto the fruit and dust over a little caster sugar. Bake for 25–30 minutes until the puddings are risen and golden. Remove and cool for about 5 minutes before tucking in. Keep any leftovers in the fridge once cooled completely for up to three days, just bring to room temperature before eating for maximum flavour.

WASTE NOT

You can use up any leftover clotted cream spooned over breakfast porridge.

Chocolate, beetroot & orange torte

I have made this torte in one form or another for many years. Pouring cream cuts the richness and, along with a coffee or healthy tisane, is perfect when the urge for something gooey overcomes you or when friends drop by for tea. It keeps for up to five days in the fridge or about three days in a cool place stored in an airtight container. Eat at room temperature.

MAKES 1 X 16CM SQUARE TORTE

butter, for greasing

1 beetroot (about 100g)

200g dark chocolate, minimum 70% cocoa solids, chopped

5 tablespoons natural yogurt

3 medium eggs

¼ teaspoon sea salt crystals

½ teaspoon natural orange extract

85g coconut palm sugar

75g ground almonds

2½ teaspoons natural beetroot powder, to dust

¾ teaspoon cocoa powder, to dust

Preheat the oven to 160°C/gas mark 3. Grease a 4cm deep, 16cm square tin with slightly sloping sides with butter and line the base and sides with baking parchment (breaking the edge by 1cm).

Peel and very finely grate the beetroot (you need 75g) and then chop even more until it's almost a pulp, put in a small bowl and set aside.

Put the chopped chocolate in a bowl large enough to sit over a small pan of gently simmering water, making sure that the base does not touch the water. Add the yogurt to the chocolate and melt together for 7 minutes. Remove the bowl from the pan of water and stir gently. When the chocolate has completely melted, stir in the beetroot pulp.

Separate the eggs into two bowls. Add salt to the whites and orange extract to the yolks. Add all but 2 tablespoons of the sugar to the yolks. Use an electric hand-held beater to whisk the whites until soft peaks form and add the remaining sugar, a tablespoon at a time, whisking well between each addition until you have stiff peaks.

Without washing the beaters, whisk the yolk mixture until pale and creamy. Fold in the beetroot and chocolate mixture. Add the ground almonds and mix until smooth. Gently fold in the egg whites until just incorporated. Pour the mixture into the prepared tin and bake for 25–30 minutes until just firm and slightly cracked on top.

Remove from the oven and leave to cool for 20 minutes before carefully lifting out of the tin with the baking parchment. Leave to cool on a wire rack. Remove the baking parchment and sift the beetroot powder and cocoa powder together and dust the torte with the mixture. Cut into as many squares as you like.

Pecan & maple syrup spongy cake

This is the perfect flourless (and fatless) sponge cake for coffee time. Served along with a scattering of blackberries and a scoop of whipped cream or yogurt, it will satisfy that after-dinner urge for a bit of sweetness. The cake also goes very nicely with a ripe pear, I would go for a dessert pear; Doyenne du Comice in preference, if you can find one, or a Beurre Hardy pear also does the job beautifully.

I find pecans the most moreish of nuts. They are full of flavoursome, heart-healthy oils and despite their fat content they don't pile on the calories.

butter, for greasing

200g pecan halves

4 medium eggs

pinch of sea salt flakes

100ml maple syrup

1 tablespoon coconut palm sugar, to dust

blackberries and whipped cream, to serve (optional)

Preheat the oven to 180°C/gas mark 4. Grease a round 20cm springform tin halfway up the sides and line with baking parchment to come 3cm up the sides.

Blitz the pecans in batches in a mini food processor or grinder until very fine, then set aside.

Separate the egg whites into a small bowl, one at a time, adding each in turn to a large bowl. This two-bowl process will prevent the yolks from contaminating the whites, which can stop them whisking to the volume you need for this cake. As you do this, pop the yolks into a medium bowl.

Whisk the whites with a pinch of salt until the whites stand firm when the whisks are lifted. Add 3 tablespoons of the maple syrup, a tablespoon at a time, and continue to whisk until the mixture is firm but not fudgy.

Without rinsing the beaters, whisk the egg yolks and the remaining maple syrup together until slightly increased in volume. Fold in all the ground pecans followed by the egg whites, carefully folding them in a third at a time. Tip into the prepared tin and bake for 30 minutes or until the cake is springy to the touch.

Turn off the oven and leave the cake in the oven for 15 minutes with the door slightly ajar. Remove from the oven and cool for 10 minutes. Remove from the tin and peel off the baking parchment and transfer to a plate. Grind the coconut palm sugar to a powder using a pestle and mortar and dust over the cake. Alternatively, put the berries on top (if using) and then dust with the sugar.

The cake keeps for 4–5 days in the fridge. Cut off a slice and bring to room temperature before eating.

Give It

Time

Tomato & cucumber salsa jelly with borage flowers

This is a good way to help use up a glut of lovely ripe red tomatoes capturing all their goodness in the jelly. For a vegetarian or vegan option, you could use agar flakes to set the jelly, just check the packet for instructions.

MAKES 2

750g very ripe tomatoes

⅛ teaspoon sea salt crystals

1⅓ organic gelatine leaves

2 teaspoons white balsamic vinegar

a few red and orange tomatoes, deseeded and chopped into tiny cubes

5cm piece of cucumber, peeled, deseeded and chopped into tiny cubes

chervil leaves, picked into small fronds, plus extra to serve

borage flowers, to serve

narrow crispy flatbreads, to serve

Chop the tomatoes roughly and purée in a food processor with the salt. Put a nylon sieve over a bowl and line with some muslin. Pour in the tomato and leave for up to 4 hours to drain. Once drained, the liquid will be quite pale. You need 225ml.

Soften the gelatine in a bowl of cold water for 5 minutes. Put a small pan over a low heat and briefly warm the vinegar with 1 tablespoon of water. Lift the gelatine into the vinegar and swirl to dissolve completely. Then add the mixture to the tomato liquid. Check for flavour, adding more salt if you like, then pour into two glasses and transfer to the fridge for about 2 hours until just starting to gel.

Mix the tomato and cucumber cubes and the chervil together to make a salsa. Gently fold the salsa into the jellies and return to the fridge until completely set.

When set, top with extra chervil and the borage flowers for prettiness and serve with crispy flatbreads.

WASTE NOT

When the correct volume of tomato water has drained off the tomatoes for the jelly, you can use any leftover liquid and the pulp to the *Rich tomato sauce* (page 127). Tomatoes and cucumber can be used for a non-spicy version of *Kachumber* (page 216).

Char siu pork with black beans

Black beans are salted fermented soybeans and give a distinctive tang to this dish; they last a while stored in an airtight jar. Rice noodles now come in exciting flavours like pumpkin with ginger, brown rice with wakami or black rice noodles and are all gluten-free so see what you can find at wholefood or health stores otherwise just use white rice noodles. The pork is good to leave in the marinade for a maximum of 24 hours but you can marinate it for less time if you like. You can also substitute the pork with firm tofu, cut into cubes and marinated in the same way as the pork and fried.

50g edamame

75g mangetout

1½ tablespoons sunflower oil

1cm piece of fresh ginger, peeled and shredded

2 garlic cloves, crushed or 2 teaspoons
   Crushed garlic (page 207)

1 small banana shallot, thinly sliced

4 spring onions, sliced diagonally

1½ tablespoons salted black beans,
   rinsed and roughly chopped

25g roasted cashews, to serve

about 85g rice noodles, cooked, to serve

some fronds of coriander, to serve

some micro purple basil leaves, to serve

FOR THE CHAR SIU PORK

150g piece pork tenderloin

2 tablespoons char siu or teriyaki marinade

1 tablespoon sesame oil

1 teaspoon ichimi togarashi

First marinate the pork. Cut the pork into about 0.5cm slices and put in a bowl with the marinade ingredients, cover with a plate and transfer to the fridge for 4–24 hours.

When ready to cook, put the edamame in a pan of boiling water and simmer for 4 minutes and drain. Shred the mangetout into long matchsticks and set aside.

Heat 1 tablespoon of the oil in a wok and stir-fry the ginger, garlic, shallot and half the spring onions for 2 minutes. Add the black beans, mangetout and edamame, stir-fry for a few seconds then tip into a bowl.

Wipe out the wok and set over a high heat then add the remaining oil. Lift the pork out of the marinade, letting any excess drip off into the bowl. Add the pork to the wok and sear for 2 minutes on each side without moving the pieces around too much. Test a piece to see if the pinkness has gone and add any marinade for the last few seconds until it bubbles. Add the vegetable mixture into the pork and stir. Remove from the heat, add the remaining spring onions and serve with the cashews, herbs and the cooked noodles.

Pea & lemon risotto with shimeji mushrooms & burrata

Buy some burrata if you are passing by a good deli on your way home and fancy a treat. Eat the other half the very next day for breakfast with some prosciutto de Parma and cooked asparagus with the best green and peppery extra virgin olive oil spooned over.

You could also make a stock from the empty pea pods that have been washed then simmered until tender. Strain off the pods, season and use the liquid right away, otherwise it turns a dark colour.

325g peas in their pods or 100g shelled peas

60g sugar snaps

2 bunches jumbo salad onions, green part only (white bulbs reserved for *Agrodolce onions* on page 123) or 1 bunch spring onions or 5 shallots, chopped

3 tablespoons olive oil

30g salted butter

75g shimeji mushrooms, trimmed and separated

500ml chicken (see page 179), vegetable or pea pod stock

2 garlic cloves, crushed to a paste with a little salt or 2 teaspoons *Crushed garlic* (page 207)

125g Arborio rice

3 tablespoons dry white wine

1 unwaxed lemon

30g finely grated fresh Parmesan

1 burrata (halved at the last minute) or 60g soft goat's cheese or curd

a handful of pea shoots

sea salt crystals and freshly ground black pepper

extra virgin olive oil, to serve

Cook the peas and sugar snaps in salted boiling water for 1 minute. Drain in a colander and refresh with cold water and slice the sugar snaps in half lengthways. Slice the onions thinly and set aside.

Heat 1 tablespoon of the oil and 5g of the butter in a frying pan and fry the mushrooms over a high heat until golden. Season and set aside.

Heat the stock in another pan until it boils. Put the remaining oil and butter in a heavy-based, medium pan over a medium heat. Sauté the sliced green onions for less than a minute then use a slotted spoon to lift the onions onto a plate, leaving the oils in the pan.

Return the pan to the heat and stir in the garlic. Add the rice and stir, then add the wine and simmer to evaporate. Start adding the stock a little at a time

letting each addition evaporate before adding more. Stir every so often until all but a spoonful of the stock remains. This should take about 20 minutes. Remove from the heat.

Finely zest the lemon into the risotto, then cut it in half and squeeze in the juice. Add the Parmesan and green onions and season to taste. Stir and put on the lid for 5 minutes. Add the last of the hot stock and the peas and sugar snaps. Stir and serve with half the burrata on top, the pea shoots, some extra virgin olive oil and a grinding of black pepper.

WASTE NOT

Any remaining mushrooms would make a lovely addition to the *Toasted sourdough with Vignotte, curly kale and mushrooms* on page 32.

Marinated herb-crusted rack of lamb

You can finish off any lamb another day with an assortment of mezze (pages 134–135). Or, prior to cooking the herb crust, cut off two cutlets and leave in the marinade. Then you can griddle them a few days later and serve with any leftover fennel and radicchio baked with Parmesan and a *Potato galette* (page 215). Griddle the cutlets for 2–3 minutes each side then leave them to rest for 5 minutes. You can accompany the whole rack or part of it on the day of roasting with fennel with radicchio and celeriac purée (page 210).

FOR THE MARINADE

450g rack of lamb or 8 ribs, French trimmed and most of the fat removed

2 garlic cloves, crushed to a paste with a little salt or 2 teaspoons *Crushed garlic* (page 207)

6 tablespoons olive oil

2 large sprigs of rosemary

8 sprigs of thyme

freshly ground black pepper and sea salt crystals

FOR THE HERB CRUST

1 slice of durum wheat Puglian bread, about 75g

1 large sprig of rosemary

5 sprigs of thyme

freshly ground black pepper and sea salt crystals

2 teaspoons Dijon mustard

Put the lamb in a deep but small ovenproof dish, smear over the garlic and add the oil, rosemary, thyme and black pepper. Massage the mixture into the lamb flesh and put in the fridge overnight or for up to 2 days.

When ready to cook, remove the lamb from the fridge 1–2 hours before cooking to bring to room temperature or put in a coolish place in the morning ready to cook later in the day. Preheat the oven to 220°C/gas mark 7. Salt the lamb flesh 20 minutes before cooking.

Meanwhile, cut the crusts off the bread, chop finely then whizz to a crumb in a mini processor. Strip the leaves from the rosemary and thyme and chop finely. Put as many crumbs as you think will be needed into a bowl (usually about 35g; use any left over – or make more – for My quick fix breakfast on page 36), mix in the herbs, a few teaspoons of the marinating oil and seasoning.

Heat a large frying pan, add a few spoons of the marinating oil and sear the lamb for 3 minutes on both sides.

Transfer to a shallow roasting tin with the herbs from the marinade and brush the fleshy side with the mustard then press on the herb crumb mixture. Roast for 15 minutes until the crumb is golden and the lamb still has a little give when pressed (if you like it less pink give it longer). Lift onto a warm plate, cover lightly with foil to rest for 10–20 minutes. Slice off what you fancy to eat right away with the suggested vegetable dishes and keep the rest, covered, in the fridge once cooled completely and use within a few days.

Rabbit rillettes with celeriac, apple & celery slaw

The secret with this recipe is not to over-salt the rabbit so you have to be a little more accurate with timings than usual. But it's well worth the effort if it makes a Frenchman smile, as indeed it did. Some classic little cornichons would be good with this as well as the slaw. Chunks of French baguette would work too but I like the crunchy contrast of the thin slices of toasted baguette. My version is a little bit chunky so if you wish you can shred the rabbit a little finer.

MAKES 1 X 300ML JAR

2 chunky rabbit legs

15g sea salt crystals

a few sprigs of rosemary and a short branch for the jar

1 teaspoon juniper berries, bruised

1 teaspoon coriander seeds

2 garlic cloves, peeled and bruised

250g goose, duck or pork fat

2½ tablespoons nibbed pistachios, roughly chopped

½ teaspoon freshly ground white pepper

thinly sliced baguette, for toasting

a few tablespoons *Poor man's capers* (page 216)

FOR THE CELERIAC, APPLE & CELERY SLAW

¼ celeriac, peeled then very thinly sliced and cut into matchsticks

1 Cox's apple, cut into quarters then thinly sliced and cut into matchsticks

a squeeze of lemon juice

1 celery stick, finely sliced diagonally

1 tablespoon good-quality mayonnaise

1 teaspoon *moutarde de Meaux* (a wholegrain mustard)

Put the rabbit legs in a small, non-corrosive dish. Rub evenly with the salt, cover and chill in the fridge for no longer than 12–14 hours.

Preheat the oven to 160°C/gas mark 3. Rinse the salt off the rabbit and dry well with kitchen paper. Place the rosemary in an enamel tin or casserole in which the rabbit legs will just fit in a single layer and put the legs on top of the rosemary. Add the juniper, coriander seeds, garlic and goose fat and cover with a double layer of foil. Cook for 40 minutes. Reduce the oven temperature to 140°C/gas mark 1 and cook for a further 55 minutes or until the bones pull out of the legs easily. Leave to rest, still covered, for 30 minutes so they don't get cold.

Put the meat in a bowl and shred with two forks. Discard the bones, cartilage and skin, which will have

fallen off, along with the herbs, spices and garlic skin, which will have fallen off. There will be juices under the goose fat. Carefully pour the fat into a jar and set aside (excellent for roasting potatoes). Pour the juices into the bowl with the meat.

Mix the pistachios and pepper into the shredded meat and tightly pack into a bowl, pot or jar and put in the fridge to set for an hour. Spoon some of the reserved goose fat over the top (just enough to cover) and top with the remaining sprig of rosemary. Store in the fridge until you want to eat it. It will keep for five days but once opened consume within two days.

To make the slaw, put the celeriac and apple in a bowl and mix in a squeeze of lemon juice to stop the apple turning brown. Add the celery and the remaining slaw ingredients and fold together to combine.

To serve, toast the baguette and eat the rillettes with the slaw and some *Poor man's capers* (page 216). A dressed salad wouldn't go amiss.

WASTE NOT

See page 210 for Waste not suggestions for celeriac.

CELEBRATE A WHOLE CHICKEN

There's that wonderful Elizabeth David recipe that all cooks know about that involves many cloves of garlic, a lemon and the best organic chicken to roast. I've made it all my cooking life, in one form or another, but its recent incarnations are versions of which I'm particularly fond as it keeps the meat so juicy and tender.

My perfect roast chicken

In the spring, when I'm lucky to have broad-leaved wild garlic with the star-shaped flower popping up amongst the bluebells in my back garden and the narrow-leaved (tricorn) garlic with delicate bell-shaped flowers in profusion on my allotment, I combine the leaves and some flowers with the last of the over-wintered rainbow chard and stuff the chicken with them all as well as ½ lemon and loads of butter.

To make a large chicken go even further, cut off one breast and a whole leg leaving the rest of the bird intact, pack the pieces into separate bags, label and freeze to use in *Roast chicken breast, tomatoes, butterbeans and Savoy cabbage* (page 94) and *Chicken with Marsala and sage* (page 41). Stuff the rest of the whole bird using this recipe or the one below with herb butter or dried seaweed flakes instead of herbs. You need a good chunky-legged, squat, plump chicken with plenty of untrimmed skin at both ends of the bird to make it easier to get the buttery herbs under the skin.

Another roast chicken

60g unsalted butter

5 sprigs of marjoram or oregano, finely chopped

10g flat-leaf parsley

zest and juice of 1 lemon

1 teaspoon pink Himalayan salt crystals, roughly crushed

1 teaspoon freshly ground black pepper

1.5–2kg organic whole chicken

4 garlic cloves

1 tablespoon olive oil

100ml white wine of choice

Preheat the oven to 200°C/gas mark 6. Squash the butter onto a plate and mix in the herbs and lemon zest and fold into the butter. Mix the pink salt and pepper together and scatter a little into the butter. With the neck end of the bird facing you, gently ease the breast skin loose with your fingers working down the legs as you go.

Take pats of the butter and squash these down where the skin is loose so it sits between the flesh and skin of the breast and legs. Season the cavity and all over the skin of the bird. Cut the lemon in half and pop into the cavity with the garlic and tie the legs loosely with string.

Put the chicken in a roasting tin, breast down, and pour over the oil, roast for 45 minutes per kilo of meat. Halfway through the roasting time, turn the bird over and spoon the oils into a bowl, leaving the juices behind, and add the wine. Baste the breast of the bird with a little of the reserved oils and continue to roast for the calculated time.

Lift the bird onto a warm plate and pour the juices into a small pan. Leave to rest, lightly covered with foil, for 20 minutes. Meanwhile, heat the juices ready to serve with the meat.

The hungry person's chicken noodle soup

350ml chicken stock

1 garlic clove, peeled

2cm fat piece of fresh ginger, peeled and roughly sliced

1 long red chilli, halved and deseeded

1 lemongrass stem, halved and bruised

about 15g coriander stems

1–2 tablespoons fish sauce

50g x 5mm wide dried rice noodles

1 pak choy, broken into whole leaves or choy sum, left whole

juice of ½ lime

leftover roast chicken, shredded off the carcass (page 176)

2–3 teaspoons sweet chilli dipping sauce

Put the stock in a pan and add the garlic, ginger, half the chilli and lemongrass. Remove the leaves from the coriander and set aside. Put the coriander stalks in the stock and add the fish sauce. Bring the mixture to the boil then simmer for 5 minutes. Shred the remaining half of the chilli and set aside for serving.

Meanwhile, put the noodles in a bowl and pour over boiling water and leave to soften for about 4 minutes.

Drain the stock into a bowl and discard the solids, return to the pan, add the pak choy and cook for a minute to just wilt. Add the lime juice, chicken and coriander leaves then drain and add the noodles. Scatter with shredded chilli and spoon over the sweet chilli dipping sauce.

Chicken risotto

Make as the recipe for the *Pea and lemon risotto with shimeji mushrooms and burrata* (page 170) but use celery and shallots instead and the stock made from the chicken carcass and bones. Shred the leftover roast chicken and add right at the end of cooking so it doesn't toughen up. Add a few handfuls of spinach to wilt into the hot risotto and freshly grated Parmesan. This is the most comforting dish partly down to the that fact you haven't wasted a scrap of that lovely bird.

Chicken stock

When you're done with the fleshy bits of your roast chicken, pick any remaining meat from the bones and put them and the broken up carcass into a pan, cover with cold water and bring to the boil. Half-cover with a lid, reduce the heat so the liquid barely moves and cook for a few hours to get a clear stock. If you want, you can add a washed, unpeeled whole onion, celery stick, bay leaf and thyme but I don't always bother. Strain and use as a cupful of tonic, a base for broth or stock for risotto. The stock will keep for four days in the fridge and also freezes well to use within a month.

Herb, garlic, orange & olive oil marinade for steak

Use this marinade for very fresh rib-eye, sirloin or fillet steak. The steaks can sit happily in the brew for 2–3 days in the fridge meaning you can shop ahead without fear your meat will spoil, just turn it daily. I cook two steaks and use one with salsa verde and the other one I use in a stir-fry of mixed vegetables the following evening, sliced and added at the end so as not to lose its pinkness.

MAKES 1–2 SERVINGS

1 large or 2 smaller rib-eye steaks, 1–1.5cm thick

4 tablespoons extra virgin olive oil

2 garlic cloves, thinly sliced

1 orange, sliced

a few sprigs of thyme

a handful of basil leaves

½ teaspoon freshly ground black pepper

sea salt crystals

Put the steak in a non-reactive dish and pour over the oil, add the garlic and orange slices and scatter with the ground pepper. Tuck the thyme and basil under and over the steaks and leave to marinate in the fridge overnight or for up to three days.

Remove the steaks from the fridge 30 minutes–1 hour before you want to cook them and salt both sides 10 minutes before cooking.

Heat a ridged griddle pan until smoking hot. Sear the steaks on one side for 2–3 minutes until browned, turn and grill the other side for 2 minutes (for rare) or cook it to your preference. Lift onto a plate, cover loosely with foil – so it doesn't steam – and leave to rest for 10–20 minutes before serving. Serve with a dressed salad and tiny boiled new potatoes or a baked potato, if you wish.

Elderflower cordial

Go out with friends and pick the very freshest elderflowers on a dry sunny day. It's best not to forage near busy roads or any obviously polluted places, but that's no fun anyway. You can pick the blooms over when you get back to the kitchen, removing all the stalks, and keep them in the fridge loosely covered in cloth overnight if you don't have enough time for the whole process. Ideally, you want the just-picked nectar freshness for the best cordial.

MAKES ABOUT 2 LITRES

1kg granulated sugar

50 or so large heads of the freshest elderflowers

65g citric acid (available from pharmacies)

2 large lemons

3 limes

Put the sugar in a large sterilised enamel, glass or china bowl and pour over 1.8 litres boiling water. Stir to dissolve the sugar, cover with a clean tea towel and leave to cool completely.

Shake the flowers to remove any hidden insects and remove any stalks. Add to the bowl with the citric acid and stir. Slice the lemons and limes and add to the bowl. Cover with a tea towel or clingfilm and leave for 36 hours in a cool, dark place.

Set a sieve over a bowl and strain the liquid off then line the sieve with a fine muslin cloth and strain the liquid again. Decant into sterilised bottles, seal and keep in the fridge for use at any time. The cordial will keep for up to a year.

Elderflower sorbet with Prosecco

MAKES ABOUT 500ML

150ml *Elderflower cordial* (see opposite)

120ml spring water

3 tablespoons icing sugar

about 375ml Prosecco (half a full bottle)

elderflower sprigs, for decoration

Mix the elderflower cordial and water together in a shallow, freezerproof container and spoon in the icing sugar. Stir and leave at room temperature until the mixture is clear – about 10 minutes. Put in the freezer overnight.

Remove from the freezer and process the mixture in a mini food processor for a few minutes until it turns white. Freeze for a minimum of 2 hours or until needed.

Scoop some sorbet into a glass and top with Prosecco and an elderflower if you have one for prettiness. There's plenty for guests and lots of Prosecco to drink.

Elderberry jelly

The shiny black berries from *Sambucus nigra* or common elder ripen between late summer and early autumn depending on the weather and how early they flowered. It is best to pick on a dry day or they can smell unappetisingly like wet dog! They are said to be good protection against flu, and birds love them, so leave plenty behind for them to feast on too. Wash the fruit-laden umbrellas well and then strip off the berries just before using.

I like to make a fresh jelly, rather than a jam-style jelly, which won't last long but just gives enough to make a few servings as a treat either for dessert with some cooked apple and a quenelle of clotted cream or for another day with a soft, smelly cheese such as Époisse or a gentler Vignotte or Chaource, a sort of take on membrillo with Manchego.

150g elderberries (about 12 umbrellas, berries stripped off)

8 teaspoons caster sugar

1 strip of orange peel

½ teaspoon organic beef gelatine powder (if using other gelatine, refer to the packet for setting instructions)

Put the berries in a pan with 2 tablespoons of cold water, the sugar and orange peel. Put the pan over a low heat for about 7 minutes to let the juice flow from the berries and dissolve the sugar. When the berries are soft, put into a nylon sieve over a measuring jug and push every drop of liquid out using a ladle; you should have about 100ml liquid.

Pour into a small pan, sprinkle the gelatine over the surface and leave to dissolve. Put over a very low heat to warm through and turn clear, swirling the pan and lifting it off the heat to prevent it from boiling or bubbling. Decant into a small container to cool completely then transfer the jelly to the fridge for a few hours or overnight to set to a jelly.

Delicious
lemon buns

These buns are great to use up lemons that are no longer fresh enough to zest easily but still have good skin. For the syrup, you can use up your old lemons that have been zested or have gone hard, even halves lurking in the fridge from the gin and tonic you had a few days back. You could also turn a few un-zestable lemons into limoncello ice. Cook an extra two as below, process them to a purée separately and add half a small bottle of vodka, extra lemon juice and caster sugar to taste. Leave to macerate for 24 hours and push through a sieve with a ladle. Spoon into a 12-hole ice cube tray to freeze and use straight up as a digestive with a little water or extra vodka.

MAKES 12 BUNS

2 unwaxed lemons

100g salted butter, cut into small cubes, plus extra for greasing

200g hazelnuts, finely ground

50g fine polenta (cornmeal)

3 tablespoons plain white spelt flour, plus extra to dust

4 medium eggs, separated

175g caster sugar

TO SERVE

lemon juice from old hard or zested lemons (juice of 2 lemons – about 4 tablespoons)

3 tablespoons caster sugar

icing sugar, to dust (optional)

Put the lemons in a pan and cover with water, bring to the boil, then reduce the heat and simmer for 20 minutes until the flesh is easily pierced with a skewer. Lift the lemons onto a plate with a slotted spoon.

Meanwhile, grease and flour a 12-hole muffin tin, tap to remove any excess flour. Cut circles of baking parchment to fit the base of each hole.

Preheat the oven to 190°C/gas mark 5.

While still hot, roughly cut up the lemons, discarding any pips. Put into a mini processor along with any juice and the butter and whizz to a fine purée – the butter should melt – then tip into a large bowl. Mix the ground hazelnuts, polenta and flour together and add to the lemon mixture.

Whisk the egg whites with electric hand-held beaters until soft peaks form, add half the caster sugar, a little at a time, and whisk between each addition until the mixture makes a glossy meringue. Without washing the beaters, whisk the yolks with the remaining caster sugar until they form a thick mousse, then whisk in the lemon mixture. If too stiff, start to use a wooden spoon to get the mixture an even consistency.

Fold in half the meringue mixture, until the mixture is smooth, then fold the remainder in gently. Spoon evenly into the prepared muffin tin and put in the oven. Reduce the temperature to 160°C/gas mark 3 and bake for 30 minutes until firm and golden.

Leave for 5 minutes then unmould onto a tray and peel off the baking parchment.

Meanwhile, make the syrup. Put the lemon and sugar in a small pan set over a low heat for the sugar to dissolve then boil for 3 minutes to a pourable syrup. While the buns are still hot, prick the surface with a skewer and pour over the syrup. Or you could forgo the syrup and sift over some icing sugar.

Raspberry & yogurt iced sherbet

'Sherbet' comes from the Arabic 'sharab' meaning a cold sweetened drink. These days it's usually a water ice containing some dairy whereas a sorbet is non-dairy.

125g raspberries

juice of ½ lemon

60g caster sugar

1 tablespoon liquid glucose

4 tablespoons natural yogurt

Blitz the raspberries with the lemon juice in a mini processor. Tip into a sieve set over a bowl and use a ladle in a circular motion to push all the juices through.

Put the sugar and glucose in a small pan with 100ml water. Set it over a low heat for 2 minutes to dissolve the sugar – it may need a swirl. Mix into the raspberry mixture and whisk in the yogurt. Transfer to a shallow container and freeze for 2 hours.

Remove from the freezer then break up the mixture with a fork and use a mini processor to break down the ice crystals. Refreeze for about 2 hours, repeat once more and freeze again.

Pop it in the fridge 15 minutes before eating if it's a bit hard to make it softly scoop-able.

Papaya, lychee, lime & coconut yogurt iced sherbet

You can find massive fat cigar-shaped papayas in Middle Eastern stores. They always seem to be riper than the small sort sold in supermarkets. They last a long time and if you know you can't manage to eat it all before it becomes over-ripe then make this iced sherbet.

Process 125g peeled flesh with half a can of drained lychees (about 100g left over from *Liquorice and coconut panna cotta* on page 194) and the juice of 1 lime.

Dissolve 60g caster sugar in 100ml water with 1 tablespoon of liquid glucose. Whisk in 3 tablespoons of coconut yogurt.

Combine everything in a freezer-proof container and freeze following the recipe for *Raspberry and yogurt iced sherbet* (see left).

Passion fruit
& raspberry
millefeuille

These little temptations aren't oversweet but carry a powerful burst of flavour. The *Passion fruit crème mousseline* (page 219) piped between the layers is a kind of enriched crème patissière and as it's tricky to make a smaller quantity you may be left with some to eat another time. Have a bit of fun and create your own decoration using a cardboard stencil. Cut out stripes or whatever design takes your fancy otherwise, simply dust the top.

MAKE 3 FOR A TEA WITH FRIENDS OR FOR SOLO MIDWEEK TREATS

90ml double cream

36 small raspberries

½ portion of *Passion fruit crème mousseline* (page 219)

FOR THE FILO CRISPS

75g salted butter

3 sheets of filo pastry

65g icing sugar

FOR THE TOPPING

icing sugar, to dust

freeze-dried raspberry powder, to dust

First make the filo crisps. Preheat the oven to 180°C/gas mark 4. Melt the butter in a small pan over a low heat and when the whey separates and sinks, pour the clear butter into a small bowl leaving the whey behind.

Turn 2 baking trays over so the flat side is uppermost and place a sheet of baking parchment over each. Lay out 1 sheet of filo on a clean work surface, brush with a third of the melted butter and sift over a third of the icing sugar in an even layer. Repeat with 2 more layers finishing with a dusting of icing sugar on the top layer.

Trim the edges straight and cut into at least 9 rectangles messuring 8 x 5cm (the quantity varies depending on the size of the filo but it's good to have leftovers). Using a palette knife, carefully lift them onto one of the parchment-covered baking trays. Cover with the other parchment-lined flat-sided baking tray so it acts like a weight. Bake for 10 minutes until evenly golden. Check and cook for longer if necessary. Leave to cool for 12 minutes before removing the top tin and parchment. When cooled completely, store the filo crisps in an airtight container.

Whisk the cream until just holding its shape. Fit a piping bag with a plain 1cm nozzle and fill with the cream. Lay 6 of the filo crisps on a work surface and pipe 3 small blobs of cream onto the centre of

each crisp, leaving plenty of space around the edges. Place 6 raspberries around the cream on each crisp, leaving space in between each raspberry for the mousseline. Squeeze out any cream left in the piping bag and spoon in the passion fruit mousseline. Pipe 6 blobs of mousseline between the raspberries.

Lay one loaded crisp on top of another to make the 3 stacks. Dust the remaining 3 filo crisps with icing sugar and, if using a stencil, lay it on top and sift over the raspberry powder.to create stripes, otherwise just dust it lightly over the icing sugar. Carefully place one on top of each stack. Put in a cool place until ready to serve.

The filo crisps will keep in an airtight container for up to a month. After assembling the millefeuille keep in the fridge and use within two days.

WASTE NOT

You should have some filo crisps left so try them with figs and Vignotte (see page 23). Any leftover filo pastry can be used to make *Pistachio tarts* (page 115). A 150ml carton of double cream will be enough for the millefeuille and crème mousseline (page 219) part of this recipe.

Chocolate, rose & pistachio bark – a fridge perk

This is a good way to use up nuts before they go stale – they don't last forever – but who needs an excuse to have this delicious chocolatey treat sitting in the fridge for a sneaky piece any time you fancy?

200g dark chocolate, minimum 70% cocoa solids, broken into small pieces

90ml double cream

30g Normandy butter with salt crystals

110g soft stoned prunes, roughly chopped

75g nibbed pistachios (or other nuts)

¼ teaspoon pul biber pepper flakes (optional)

30g crystallised rose petals, chopped if large

5 amaretti, quartered

raw cocoa powder, to dust (optional)

Take a saucepan and fill with 3cm water and bring to a gentle simmer. Put the chocolate, cream and butter in a heatproof bowl large enough to sit in the pan without the base touching the water. Heat the chocolate mixture for 5 minutes. Remove the bowl from the pan and leave for about 4 minutes before stirring to melt all the ingredients together. Fold in the prunes, pistachios, pul biber, if using, crystallised rose petals and amaretti.

Line a shallow tray approx. 15 x 25cm with foil to come up the sides a little. Tip the mixture into it and use a spatula to spread the mixture evenly to fill the tray. Leave to cool completely then chill for at least 3 hours or overnight. Dust with raw cocoa powder, if using, and it's ready for eating.

Slice off thin slivers to eat at any time.

Liquorice & coconut panna cotta with lychees

The intense aniseed flavour of ground liquorice root is tempered with white chocolate and rich coconut cream. Scented lychees go so well with this exciting pudding as do blood oranges when in season. Liquorice powder is available online and in wholefood and health shops.

250ml carton of coconut cream

1½ teaspoons liquorice powder

35g white chocolate

1½ gelatine leaves

200g canned lychees, drained

Put the coconut cream in a small pan over a low heat for 8 minutes. Add the liquorice powder and whisk to break up any lumps. Smash the chocolate into small squares and add to the pan then remove from the heat and leave to melt without stirring.

Meanwhile, soak the gelatine leaves in cold water for 5 minutes to soften. Squeeze and add to the pan.

Whisk the mixture until smooth and divide between two 125ml upright metal dariole mouldsor espresso cups. Leave to cool completely then chill in the fridge overnight to set. To serve, dip the base of the moulds in hot water for a few seconds and invert onto a plate. Serve with a few lychees.

WASTE NOT

Canned lychees go so well with this panna cotta and you can use up the rest of the can to make the *Papaya, lychee, lime and coconut yogurt iced sherbet* on page 188.

Those Little

Extras

'Luxury is not a necessity to me, but beautiful and good things are.'

—

Anaïs Nin

Tapenade

The added hint of fennel is not classically an ingredient in tapenade but it really brings out the other flavours. This recipe is to be used for *Sardines on toast* (page 29). You could also use it for a little snack when exhaustion overcomes. Pick up some charcuterie on the way home, get out the jar of *Grilled marinated peppers* (page 200), pop some Middle Eastern flatbreads into a hot oven and serve along with a bowl of this tapenade and enjoy.

125g Kalamata olives

25g capers, drained if brined or rinsed if salted

1 small garlic clove, crushed to a paste with a little salt or a small spoonful of *Crushed garlic* (page 207)

4 anchovy fillets

2 pinches of pul biber pepper flakes

¼ teaspoon fennel liqueur or a pinch of pollen (optional)

3–4 tablespoons extra virgin olive oil

a few marjoram or oregano sprigs, chopped

Pit the olives and roughly chop. Put them in a mini food processor with all the other ingredients except the oil and marjoram and blitz together. Add the oil, a tablespoon at a time, blitzing in between until you are happy with the texture (I like mine a little chunky). Stir in the marjoram and eat straightaway or store in the fridge for up to five days in a screw-top jar.

Chilli & garlic oil

Use the oil to make a spicy dressing by whisking in lime or lemon juice to use with baked fish and cooked noodles or pasta with a can of tuna folded in.

100ml olive oil

1 garlic clove, crushed with a little salt or 1 teaspoon *Crushed garlic* (page 207)

1 large red chilli, deseeded and chopped

finely grated zest of 1 unwaxed lime or lemon

freshly ground black pepper

Put the oil, garlic, chilli and lemon zest in a small saucepan over a very low heat for just over a minute. Season with pepper and cool completely. Put in a screw-top jar. This should keep for up to a month.

Grilled marinated peppers

I like these with grilled radicchio, a piece of creamy burrata and the oil from their jar spooned over. Scatter with some extra Urfa pepper, the Turkish sweet, fruity, dark purple capsicum flakes. These are a quirky ingredient to have in your store cupboard.

4 large red Romano peppers

extra virgin olive oil, to cover

1 small garlic clove crushed with a little salt or 1 teaspoon *Crushed garlic* (page 207)

a few sprigs of rosemary

freshly ground black pepper

2 pinches of Urfa pepper flakes (optional)

Preheat a grill to high and arrange the rack about 15cm from the heat. Line a tray with foil and lay the peppers on top. Grill for about 8 minutes until the skins blister and blacken a little. Turn them over and cook for a further 5 minutes. Tip them into a large bowl and cover with a pan lid or tray and leave to cool completely.

Put a dash or two of oil in a bowl and mix in the garlic and rosemary. Peel the peppers, discarding the skin and seeds, then lay them in the oil and garlic. Add a pinch of black pepper and scatter with the Urfa pepper if using. Transfer to a screw-top jar with a secure lid, add enough oil to cover and put in the fridge to marinate. The peppers will keep for up to three weeks.

Toasted sesame seeds

Toast 50g sesame seeds at a time. Put in a frying pan over a medium heat and dry-toast the sesame seeds, stirring with a wooden spoon for 8–10 minutes until golden. Tip onto a plate lined with kitchen paper. Spread them out and when cold tip into a screw-top jar. They keep on the shelf or in the cupboard for a few months.

Toasted pine nuts

Toast 100g pine nuts at a time. Put ½ teaspoon of sunflower oil in a frying pan along with the pine nuts. Place over a medium heat and stir with a wooden spoon for 2 minutes – don't leave them or you get patchy burnt bits. Tip onto a plate lined with kitchen paper and rub with more kitchen paper to get the dusty residue off the nuts. Leave to cool completely then tip into a screw-top jar. They will keep for up to a few weeks on the shelf or in the cupboard.

Tarragon & hazelnut pesto

This pesto is for use in the *Roast chicken breast* recipe on page 94, or tossed through pasta for a quick and simple meal, or use in *Ali's quick fix of ravioli, courgette and goat's cheese* (page 64) .

20g tarragon

2 tablespoons skinned hazelnuts, lightly toasted and roughly crushed

2 garlic cloves, crushed with a little salt or 2 teaspoons *Crushed garlic* (page 207)

a small pinch of coconut palm sugar

2 large pinches of freshly ground black pepper

75ml extra virgin olive oil

25g Parmesan, freshly grated

Strip the tarragon leaves off the stems straight into a mini food processor or blender. Add the hazelnuts, garlic, sugar, pepper and oil and blitz to your preferred texture. (This often depends on the use you have in mind for it). Tip into a small dish and fold in the Parmesan, smooth the top and pour over a slick of olive oil, to cover (this helps to keep it longer and prevent it from losing its gorgeous bright green colour).

The pesto will last in the fridge for a few days or freeze for up to a week.

Cashew aioli

Try this deliciously different take on classic aioli with *Tray-roasted vegetables* (page 89) or *Pumpkin and cavolo nero with goat's cheese and polpetti* (page 90). You'll need to soak the cashews overnight before making this.

100g raw cashews

2 teaspoons Dijon mustard

1 teaspoon honey

2 garlic cloves, crushed to a paste with a little salt or 2 teaspoons *Crushed garlic* (page 207)

juice of 1 lemon

50ml extra virgin olive oil

50ml olive oil

sea salt crystals, to taste

Soak the cashews in cold water overnight in the fridge.

The next day, drain then whizz the cashews to a purée in a mini food processor with the mustard, honey, garlic, half the lemon juice and a spoonful of the extra virgin olive oil. Add the remaining oil a little at a time so the mixture emulsifies. Add the remaining lemon juice and salt to taste; if it's too stiff whisk in a splash of water. Keeps in the fridge for up to four days.

Crispy capers

You can make these a few hours before you need them or the day before. Use in *Pear, watercress, beetroot and Gorgonzola salad with hazelnuts* (page 20) and *Sobrasada on toast* (page 28). These are so versatile you can sprinkle them over whatever you fancy.

5 tablespoons capers in brine

5 tablespoons olive oil

Rinse and dry the capers really well and leave to air dry for as long as possible.

Heat the oil in a frying pan, add the capers and fry over a high heat until crisp, shaking the pan from time to time. Keep a close eye on the pan so that it doesn't smoke too much. Remove from the heat and tip onto a plate lined with kitchen paper and leave to cool completely. Put in a screw-top jar.

Crispy shallots

There's nothing like the taste of homemade crispy-fried shallots kept in a quirky jar in the larder ready to scatter and add a touch of flavoursome crunch to whatever you fancy from eggs to rice, and curries to salads. They will keep for a month or even longer stored in a screw-top jar and take about 15 minutes of zen-like attention. It's very therapeutic gently stirring them as they turn a lovely golden brown.

200ml sunflower oil

7 banana shallots, peeled and thinly sliced

Before you start frying, put a metal sieve (not nylon as it will melt) over a bowl and line both the sieve and a plate with kitchen paper.

Heat a large wok over a medium heat, add the oil and shallots, reduce the heat to low and fry them, stirring regularly, until an even golden colour. The art is to stop when there are still some paler golden pieces running through that aren't too dark.

When the shallots are done, pour them and the oil into the prepared sieve then tip the drained shallots onto the lined plate and spread out to cool and crisp up. When they have cooled completely, pop them into a screw-top jar and store on the shelf or in the cupboard. Recycle the oil for use another time.

Crispy ginger strands

Use mixed with crispy-fried shallots to add a flourish to seared scallops, soups or any Asian-inspired dish.

25g piece of fresh ginger

6 tablespoons sunflower oil

sea salt flakes

Peel the ginger and use a very sharp knife to cut it into wafer thin slices. Pile up the slices a few at a time, slice into fine matchsticks and pat dry with kitchen paper. Heat the oil in a small pan over a low heat and fry the ginger in two batches, stirring until golden and crisp. Put a metal sieve (not nylon as it will melt) over a bowl and line both the sieve and a plate with kitchen paper.

When the ginger is golden, pour it and the oil into the sieve, then tip the ginger onto the lined plate and spread out to cool. Return the oil to the pan and fry the second batch. When cold, transfer the strands to a screw-top jar. They will keep for a few weeks stored on a shelf or in a cupboard. Toss with a few sea salt flakes before using.

Curly kale ash

Use dusted over pasta dishes, cooked fish or roasted vegetables, or mix into the *Dukka* on page 208 for an extra spark of green.

a large handful of green curly kale, thick stems removed

Preheat the oven to 180°C/gas mark 4 and put the kale on a baking tray large enough to hold the kale in a single layer. Bake for 5 minutes. Reduce the heat to 110°C/gas mark ¼ and dry it out for a further 5 minutes or until it crumbles easily but is still bright green. Leave it to cool completely then use your hands to scrunch the kale up to a powder. Store in a screw-top jar for up to a month. Keep some of the whole pieces to eat right away as a nibble scattered with sea salt crystals or one of the Mixed salts (page 208).

Quick kimchi

Use for *Bulgogi beef* (page 141).

½ Chinese leaf cabbage, cut in half lengthways

4 tablespoons brown rice vinegar

4 teaspoons sunflower oil

2 teaspoons sesame oil

2 tablespoons coconut palm sugar

2cm piece of fresh ginger, peeled, finely sliced and chopped

1 large red chilli, deseeded and finely chopped

2 spring onions, finely sliced

Cut the cabbage into 3cm chunks and blanch in a large pan of boiling water for 20 seconds only. Drain and refresh under cold running water then drain again. Measure the rice vinegar into a non-corrosive bowl and mix in the remaining ingredients. Fold in the cabbage, cover and chill for at least 3 hours or up to three days.

Smoky caramelised hazelnuts

If 'smoky' doesn't appeal to you, use pul biber (sweet pepper also known as Aleppo pepper) instead of the smoked paprika or use crushed cumin or coriander seeds. Use in *Pear, watercress, beetroot and Gorgonzola salad with hazelnuts* (page 20). You could also crunch some up and scatter over *Paprika and salt-crusted monkfish and padrón pepper skewers* (page 104).

50g skinned hazelnuts

1½ teaspoons coconut palm sugar, crushed to a powder

¼ teaspoon smoked hot paprika

Preheat the oven to 140°C/gas mark 2. Line an oven sheet with foil, add all the ingredients along with 1½ teaspoons water and toss well. Bake for 5 minutes. Turn the hazelnuts to coat and cook for a further 5 minutes. They should be hard and crispy and loose on the tray. If not, loosen and leave on the tray to cool. Transfer to a screw-top jar. These will keep for a good few weeks.

A whole head of crushed garlic

Having a jar of crushed garlic on hand, as and when I need it, is a real time-saver as I love garlic and use a lot in my recipes. It's so quick and easy to prepare in advance with the help of a strong cook's knife or you could grate it onto the salt. In general, where a recipe calls for two large garlic cloves, use two teaspoons of this garlic paste.

1 head of garlic, choose one with firm plump cloves

1½ teaspoons sea salt crystals

oil of choice (olive, extra virgin olive oil, sunflower, rapeseed oil), to cover

Break up the whole head of garlic and cut the root ends from each clove. Smash lightly with the blade of a heavy cook's knife to loosen the skin so it falls off.

Make a pile of salt on the chopping board to catch the juices and grate the garlic over using the fine holes on a box grater or Microplane. Use your knife to crush the garlic and salt together until you have a paste. If you want a less smooth result, thinly slice the cloves then finely chop and crush into the salt with the heavy knife blade – it takes longer but I like to do it this way.

Put in a small screw-top jar with a secure lid, cover with oil by 1cm and store in the fridge for up to a week.

Mustard & white balsamic vinaigrette

Use *Raspberry vinegar* (page 213) for a bit of pink fun, it's an exciting flavour and great colour for some dishes. You can substitute the Dijon mustard with wholegrain mustard if you like. If you want to double the quantity only use 2 teaspoons of mustard.

1½ teaspoons Dijon mustard

1 tablespoon white balsamic vinegar

tiny pinch of sea salt crystals

3 tablespoons extra virgin olive oil

Put the mustard, vinegar and salt in a screw-top jar with a secure lid and mix them together. Add the oil, tightly screw on the lid and shake vigorously to emulsify. The vinaigrette keeps for up to five days in the fridge.

Dukka

As with many spicy Middle Eastern blends each dukka varies slightly from household to market stall. So in keeping with tradition this is my version. Dip Arabic bread into peppery cold-pressed olive oil then into this coarse dukka mix and have a few olives too. Or use as a sprinkle to add crunch to dishes like *Ali's quick fix* (page 64).

20g shelled pistachios

20g skinned hazelnuts

15g coriander seeds

10g cumin seeds

2 tablespoons bright green pistachio nibs (optional)

15g *Toasted pine nuts* (page 200), (optional)

20g *Toasted sesame seeds* (page 200)

1 teaspoon freshly ground black pepper

sea salt crystals, to serve

Preheat the oven to 180°C/gas mark 4. Put the shelled pistachios (not the nibs) and hazelnuts on a baking tray, keeping them separate. Roast for 8–10 minutes and tip onto a plate lined with kitchen paper and leave to cool completely.

Coarsely crush the hazelnuts using a pestle and mortar then add the pistachios and pound to a crunchy loose texture. (Don't over pound the nuts otherwise their oils will turn the mixture into a paste.)

Put the coriander and cumin seeds in a dry frying pan over a low–medium heat and stir constantly for 2 minutes until aromatic. Tip onto a plate lined with kitchen paper and cool. Whizz until fine in a spice grinder. Add to the nuts.

Next, grind the pistachio nibs and toasted pine nuts roughly and add to the mixture. Roughly whizz the toasted sesame seeds in the grinder and add, along with the pepper. Store in a screw-top jar where it will keep on the shelf or in the cupboard for a few months. Just before using the dukka, add the sea salt crystals.

Mixed salts

Have fun with salt mixtures to have on hand to add a flourish to a dish. Experiment with many more flavour combinations depending on what herbs you have growing – you can add them fresh or dried – and keep a look out for interesting salts in specialist stores or online.

Cornish sea salt flakes, finely grated zest of an unwaxed lemon, a pinch of smoked paprika and dried chilli flakes.

Persian blue salt crystals, finely grated zest of a well-washed orange, crushed coriander seeds.

Himalayan pink salt crystals, roughly crushed fennel seeds, fennel pollen or flower buds.

Celariac purée

Use this and the adjacent recipe as an accompaniment to *Marinated herb-crusted rack of lamb* (page 173).

450g or ½ large celeriac

a knob of butter

1 tablespoon olive oil

1 teaspoon sea salt crystals and freshly ground black pepper

extra virgin olive oil, to serve

Peel and chop the celeriac into 3cm pieces, put in a pan, cover with cold water and add salt. Bring to the boil, half cover with a lid, reduce the heat to a simmer and cook for about 12 minutes until soft.

Drain off all but 3 tablespoons of water, add the butter and olive oil, cover completely, reduce the heat to very low and cook for another 5 minutes. Purée in a mini processor and serve with a slick of extra virgin olive oil.

WASTE NOT

To use up any leftover celeriac purée, you can make a very simple dish with a rich flavour, which really works as a leftover snack. Put the remaining celeriac in a bowl, make a well in the centre, break in 2–3 quail eggs and steam for 4 minutes. Remove from the heat, add a trickle extra virgin olive oil and leave for 2 minutes before digging in. Scatter with *Crispy shallots* and dust with *Curly kale ash* for extra flavour (pages 202 and 204).

Braised fennel with trevise

250g fennel

1 tablespoon olive oil

a large knob of salted butter

100g trevise or radicchio

freshly ground black pepper

Slice the fennel into 6 wedges lengthways and put in a pan with the oil over a medium heat to sear on all sides until just golden. Add the butter and as soon as it sizzles add a splash of water, then clamp on the lid straightaway to capture the steam. Braise for 3 minutes over a low heat. Slice the trevise into quarters lengthways, add to the fennel and cook for a further 2 minutes. Season with pepper and serve.

WASTE NOT

If you have any fennel left over and a bit of kale in the fridge then you can fold the kale through the fennel and trevise and pop everything into a gratin dish. Smother with pecorino nero or Parmesan and bake in a very hot oven until golden, making this a great quick fix supper dish to be served with a piece of fish or steak. Trevise or radicchio can be used *Smashed potatoes, chicken balls, crispy gremolata and radicchio* (pages 96–97).

Za'atar

Za'atar is an Arabic wild thyme and is how
this Middle Eastern mix came to be named.
I have always made my own za'atar with a
garden mix of dried thyme, marjoram in
flower and summer savory. Make crispbread
from flatbreads or pitta bread. Simply mix
a bit of za'atar with a good glug of olive oil.
Paint the mixture over one side of the bread
and put in a moderate oven (180°C/gas mark
4) to crisp up for about 6 minutes. Serve with
olives and feta or labneh (*Pickled cucumber
with dill labneh* on page 128). You could also
use it scattered over *Tray-roasted vegetables* on
page 89.

20g *Toasted sesame seeds* (page 200)

10g sumac

2–3 tablespoons home-dried mix of thyme,
  marjoram and summer savory

Mix all the ingredients together in a bowl and
transfer to a screw-top jar. It will keep for a few
months stored on the shelf or in the cupboard.

Yuzu pickled red cabbage

A little of this is delicious with cold roast chicken or cold fatty belly pork and also with a good charcuterie platter. Yuzu juice is now widely available in bottles and hopefully whole fruits will be coming soon. The slightly lumpy fruit, which looks a little like a mandarin, is a tangy cross between a lemon, orange and grapefruit with a lime hit too. Ichimi togarashi is the Japanese hot chilli pepper.

½ red cabbage

1 tablespoon sea salt crystals

3 tablespoons yuzu juice (use fresh when available)

3 tablespoons brown rice vinegar

2 tablespoons coconut palm sugar, roughly crushed

½ teaspoon ichimi togarashi

Cut the cabbage in half and shred very finely using a mandolin or a very sharp knife. Put in a bowl with the salt. Use your hands to massage the salt into the cabbage until it feels as though it has dissolved. Cover and leave for about 6 hours.

Rinse the salt off the cabbage and put back into the bowl. Add the yuzu, vinegar, sugar, 125ml cold water and the ichimi togarashi. Pack into a screw-top jar and leave to pickle. Store in the fridge where it will keep for up to two months.

Raspberry vinegar

When raspberries are cheap and at their peak, or you have grown your own, even if you have a few left in the fridge that need using up, make this to bottle up for home use or to give as a present. It's a stunning colour with a good flavour.

MAKES 500ML

100g raspberries or as many as you have spare

500ml white balsamic vinegar

2 tablespoons unrefined caster sugar

Put the raspberries in a glass jar with a lid and squash them with a fork. Add the vinegar and sugar, cover and leave to macerate for about four days or until a bright pink colour. Pour into a muslin-lined sieve set over a non-reactive saucepan and let it drip through until just the pulp remains in the muslin; it takes a few hours. Put the pan over a medium heat and simmer the liquid for 8 minutes.

Pour the raspberry vinegar into a sterilised jar or bottle using a funnel, if you have one, and store in a cool, dark place. It will be ready to use after a week and lasts for a few months.

Potato galettes

Simply served with baked fish and a fresh green salad, these potato galettes are wonderful. They will keep for a couple of days in the fridge and freeze well. I sometimes like them just on their own with a good dressed salad, nothing could be nicer for a fast supper.

MAKES 4

450g Désirée potatoes, peeled or unpeeled

25g salted butter, melted

sea salt crystals and freshly ground black pepper

Preheat the oven to 200°C/gas mark 6.

Use a mandoline or a very sharp knife to slice the potatoes thinly. Put a third of the potatoes in a bowl, season lightly and add some of the butter. Repeat twice. Mix with your hands and then layer up into four round tins measuring 2cm x 10cm or use Yorkshire pudding trays and cook for about 40 minutes until sizzling and golden on top. Unmould with the help of a spatula. Eat one or two right away and leave the remainder to cool completely. They will keep in the fridge for a day or two.

WASTE NOT

Any leftovers can be heated the next or following day in an oven preheated to 220°C/gas mark 7. Place the potato cakes on a foil-lined tray and put into the oven for 10 minutes, cover if over-browning. Eat with poached eggs, grilled pancetta, and wilted spinach or the *Marinated herb-crusted rack of lamb* (page 173) or *My perfect roast chicken* (page 176).

Shaved potato crisps

1 medium potato (Désirée or King Edward)

1 teaspoon olive oil

sea salt crystals or *Mixed salts* (page 208), to serve

Preheat the oven to 160°C/gas mark 3. Use a vegetable peeler to thinly shave the potato, rinse and dry well.

Line a large oven tray with baking parchment, add the oil and the potato, toss well and arrange in a single layer fairly spaced out. Bake for 10 minutes – it's good to open the oven door a couple of times to let the steam escape as the crisps are drying out. Remove from the oven and scrape them loose with a palette knife, turning them as you go. Return to the oven and crisp them for a further 10 minutes. Toss with salt while hot and eat right away as a snack while your meal is cooking.

Poor man's capers

These pickled nasturtium seeds couldn't be simpler to prepare. You just have to grow nasturtiums, which isn't hard to do as you reap the benefits by having the leaves, flowers then the seeds to harvest. Once they like your garden or window box nothing stops them. From spring through to the first frost they will offer you something to lift a dish.

Keep a small jar of white balsamic vinegar mixed with 1 teaspoon of caster sugar in the fridge, and as you find the seeds on the plants wash them well and add them to the jar. They will keep for months and are delicious scattered over salads or with a selection of charcuterie or with *Rabbit rillettes with celeriac, apple and celery slaw* on page 174.

Kachumber

You could make a less spicy variation of this salsa to serve with leftover roast chicken. Just add some chopped Lebanese cucumber, leave out the mustard seeds, cumin and chilli powder, using a pinch or two of pul biber pepper flakes instead, along with herbs such as oregano and parsley.

This version of Kachumber goes particularly well with the *Shami kebabs* on page 146.

2cm piece of fresh ginger

4 radishes, finely diced

1 medium tomato, quartered, deseeded and diced

¼ pink or red onion, finely chopped

1 large red chilli, deseeded and finely chopped

a few mint sprigs, leaves torn

½ teaspoon yellow mustard seeds

1 teaspoon sunflower oil

pinch of freshly ground cumin seeds

pinch of Kashmiri chill powder

juice of 1 lime

Grate the ginger and squeeze the juice from the grated pulp into a bowl and add the radishes, tomato, onion and chilli and throw in the mint. Use a pestle and mortar to crush the mustard seeds finely, stir in the oil, add the cumin seeds and the chilli powder and squeeze over the lime juice. Mix well and serve immediately.

Meringue shards

These make a lovely sweet treat served with the remains of the passion fruit crème mousseline (see opposite) or try them dusted with dried passion fruit or raspberry powder and serve with fresh raspberries for a quick dessert.

65g caster sugar

1 egg white

Preheat the oven to 130°C/gas mark 1. Put the sugar and 2 tablespoons of water into a small saucepan and gently heat to dissolve the sugar. Increase the heat and boil until the mixture reaches 121°C on a sugar thermometer.

Meanwhile, use an electric hand beater to whisk the egg white to soft peaks. Pour the hot syrup onto the white while still whisking to make a meringue. Carry on whisking until the meringue has cooled right down and is very stiff.

Line two baking trays with baking parchment and put a small dab of the meringue under each corner to keep the parchment in place. Using a palette knife, smear the meringue mixture into flat oblong shapes measuring about 15 x 7cm – they don't need to be perfect as the imperfections add character to the shards.

Bake for about 1 hour until pale in colour. (They will seem soft but they will crisp up as they cool.) Remove from the oven and leave them to cool for 2 minutes before gently easing them off the paper. When completely cold, put the shards in an airtight container layered between sheets of baking parchment where they will keep for weeks.

Passion fruit crème mousseline

100g good-quality white chocolate, broken into squares

20g salted butter, cut into small cubes

60ml double cream

9 passion fruit

about 50ml shop-bought passion fruit juice or orange juice

1 large egg yolk

25g caster sugar

2 teaspoons cornflour

Put the chocolate, butter and cream in a heatproof bowl large enough to sit over a pan of barely simmering water so its base doesn't touch the water. Heat for 4 minutes. Remove the pan from the heat, remove the bowl, stir well to melt completely and set aside.

Cut the passion fruit in half and scoop the flesh out into a mini processor or blender. Whizz to loosen the pulp from the seeds (you don't want to crush the seeds.) Pour into a sieve set over a measuring jug and use a ladle in a circular motion to push through all the pulp. Top up with enough bought juice to bring the volume up to 150ml.

Mix the yolk, sugar and cornflour in a small bowl, add 1 tablespoon of the above juice mixture and whisk to combine. Put the remaining juice mixture in a small pan. Place the pan over a low heat for 2 minutes then add the egg mixture, whisking constantly for about 2 minutes to thicken. Pour it into the melted chocolate mixture, stir well, cover with clingfilm and cool completely before chilling in the fridge for 3 hours or overnight. This keeps for up to 3 days or freezes well.

INDEX

221

SUPPLIERS

www.thegreenseedcompany.com for organic edible flower seeds

www.unwins.co.uk
for mizuna, rockets, micro leaves

www.justseaweed.com for dulse

www.clearspring.co.uk for hijiki

www.coyo.co.uk for pure coconut yogurt

tofuking (UK)Ltd for non GM Yuba

www.crostamollica.com for pane Pugliese

www.allthingsliquorice.co.uk for fine liquorice powder

www.merchant-gourmet.com for beluga lentils

www.souschef.co.uk for Espelette pepper, dried fruit powders, salts, dried marigold petals

www.buywholefoodsonline.co.uk for beetroot powder

www.biona.co.uk for organic coconut palm sugar

www.wildflowershop.co.uk for salad burnet

www.plant-theatre.com for edible flower and salad kits

www.naturesbest.co.uk for raw cashews

www.naturescape.co.uk for wild garlic

www.korewildfruitnursery.co.uk
for narrow-leaved garlic

www.soilassociation.org

www.foe.co.uk

ACKNOWLEDGEMENTS

Thank you to Kyle for giving me the chance to write *Solo*. A massive thanks to Ali Allen, firstly for instilling the idea in our heads that Solo was a creative and really useful project to immerse ourselves in. For her stylish and beautiful propping and images throughout. Her generous giving of precious time, commitment and great company. Vicky Orchard, my editor, who with much patience and understanding got us there smiling in the end. Also thanks to all the team at Kyle Books. Thanks to Alice for her timeless *Solo* design. A special thanks to Roisin Nield for being such a great friend, her massive support way beyond the call of duty getting us sorted. My gentle, hard-working assistant, Elisa Crestani. Clare Whittingham, for librarian skills. Karl Rixon, for valiantly humping heavy props around the place. My sons, Dan and Ben, Ellie de Rose and Angie Abramovich for being encouraging and enthusiastic eaters of my food. Simon Tubby for talented advice, Angela Dukes of *Food and Travel* for encouragement. Lesley Faddy for always having an answer. To Ireen Esmann for pretty bantam eggs. And thank you to Sir Roy Strong for allowing me to use his quote I heard on *Desert Island Discs* for the sake of art!